The Best of The Mailbox
Bulletin Boards Book 2

W9-CFX-954

Table of Contents

About This Book

Packed with loads of our most popular bulletin boards for intermediate teachers, **The Best of** The **Mailbox® Bulletin Boards • Book 2** is the perfect resource for creating an inviting classroom! Inside you'll find more than 100 motivating and easy-to-create displays compiled from The Mailbox® line of magazines and books.

Organized by season, this handy resource includes displays for fall, winter, spring, and a special collection for any day of the year. A wide array of patterns accompany the boards, saving you valuable time in creating and setting up your displays. Use the boards to supplement instruction, manage your classroom, and display student work. **The Best of** The Mailbox® **Bulletin Boards • Book 2** is the best resource for an eye-catching classroom!

Managing Editor: Debra Liverman
Editor at Large: Diane Badden
Copy Editors: Tazmen Carlisle, Amy Kirtley-Hill, Karen L. Mayworth, Kristy Parton, Debbie Shoffner, Cathy Edwards Simrell
Art Coordinators: Theresa Lewis Goode, Stuart Smith
Artists: Pam Crane, Theresa Lewis Goode, Clevell Harris, Ivy L. Koonce, Clint Moore, Greg D. Rieves, Rebecca Saunders, Barry Slate, Stuart Smith, Donna K. Teal
The Mailbox® Books.com: Judy P. Wyndham (MANAGER); Jennifer Tipton Bennett (DESIGNER/ARTIST); Karen White (INTERNET COORDINATOR); Paul Fleetwood, Xiaoyun Wu (SYSTEMS)

President, The Mailbox Book Company™: Joseph C. Bucci
Director of Book Planning and Development: Chris Poindexter
Curriculum Director: Karen P. Shelton
Book Development Managers: Cayce Guiliano, Elizabeth H. Lindsay, Thad McLaurin
Editorial Planning: Kimberley Bruck (MANAGER); Debra Liverman, Sharon Murphy, Susan Walker (TEAM LEADERS)
Editorial and Freelance Management: Karen A. Brudnak; Sarah Hamblet, Hope Rodgers (EDITORIAL ASSISTANTS)
Editorial Production: Lisa K. Pitts (TRAFFIC MANAGER); Lynette Dickerson (TYPE SYSTEMS); Mark Rainey (TYPESETTER)
Librarian: Dorothy C. McKinney

©2003 by THE EDUCATION CENTER, INC.
All rights reserved.
ISBN# 1-56234-577-X

Manufactured in the United States
10 9 8 7 6 5 4 3 2 1

Fall

Take a giant step toward welcoming your new class with the fancy footwork of this display! On colorful paper, copy a class supply of the **sock pattern** (page 77). Also make a class supply of the **sneaker pattern** (page 77) on white paper. Glue a student's school picture (cut from last year's yearbook) on each sock. Then staple the socks to the display. On the first day, have each child decorate a sneaker pattern and then staple it atop his sock. Makes a "socks-sational" door display too!

J. Royce Brunk, Seoul Foreign School, Seoul, Korea

Let your new students know they can bank on a great year! For each child, copy the **bill pattern** (page 78) on green paper. Cut out the center oval; then tape a photo of the new student behind it and post as shown. Add a border of pink **piggy bank patterns** (page 78) on which students have written paragraphs describing their hopes for the school year or how they'd spend $1,000.

Karen Maresca—Gr. 6, St. Vincent de Paul School, Stirling, NJ

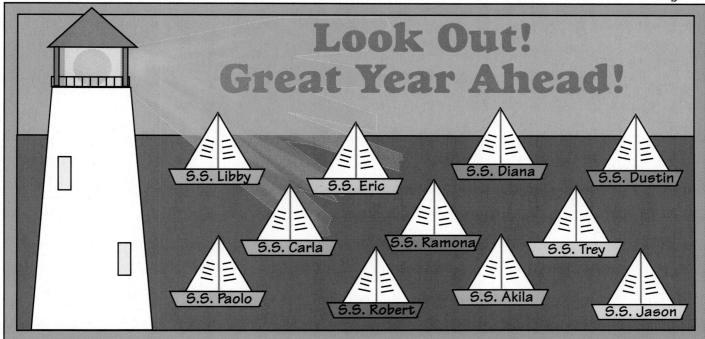

Enlarge the **lighthouse pattern** (page 79) and post it on a background of light and dark blue paper as shown. Add beams of light with yellow chalk. Have each student fold up and glue down the bottom inch or two of a white paper triangle. After labeling and coloring the boat's bottom as shown, have the student draw a vertical line on the sail and label it with words to describe herself. Have students use the words later in descriptive paragraphs about themselves.

adapted from an idea by Colleen Dabney—Grs. 6–7, Williamsburg Christian Academy, Williamsburg, VA

Pep up a back-to-school discussion of class rules by posting the **cheerleader pattern** (page 80) on a board as shown. Ask students to brainstorm a list of elements needed for a safe, happy, and productive school year; then have each student write a short cheer on a pennant-shaped cutout. Post the pennants, adding tissue paper pom-poms to the corners of each. Use the display as a springboard to a discussion of class rules for the year.

Tina Genay—Gr. 4, Winchester School District, Winchester, VA
Ann Wasko—Gr. 4, Windsor School District, Windsor, NY

For a "tree-riffic" back-to-school display, mount a large tree trunk labeled as shown on a bulletin board. Add a green body of leaves labeled with the names of your new students. Also add to the display an enlarged copy of the **squirrel pattern** (page 81). During the second week of school, select one student to highlight. Copy a supply of the **nut pattern** (page 81) on light brown construction paper. Give a pattern to each child to fill in with a compliment about the student of the week. Pin the nut cutouts along the base of the tree. At the end of the week, send the cutouts home with the special student; then select a new student to feature the following week. Continue until all students have been honored.

Eileen James—Grs. 3–4
St. Matthews Elementary
Louisville, KY

Welcome students back with a display that spotlights your school's staff! Cut faculty photos from an old school yearbook. Glue each photo to an unlined index card as shown. Add each coworker's name and job on the card to resemble a stamped envelope. Post the cards with a large **mailbox pattern** (page 82). Use this idea to welcome your first-class students back to school too!

Karen Bryant, Rosa Taylor Elementary, Macon, GA

Looking for an "ap-peeling" display for back-to-school? Post a large tree shape cut from butcher paper as shown. Give each student a copy of an **apple pattern** (page 83) to label with a word of wisdom about how to succeed in school. After the child has colored his apple, have him staple the cutout to the tree. Use the tree year-round by giving students a new set of seasonal cutouts and a new writing topic at the start of each month.

Kim Myers—Gr. 5
Albert Harris Elementary
Martinsville, VA

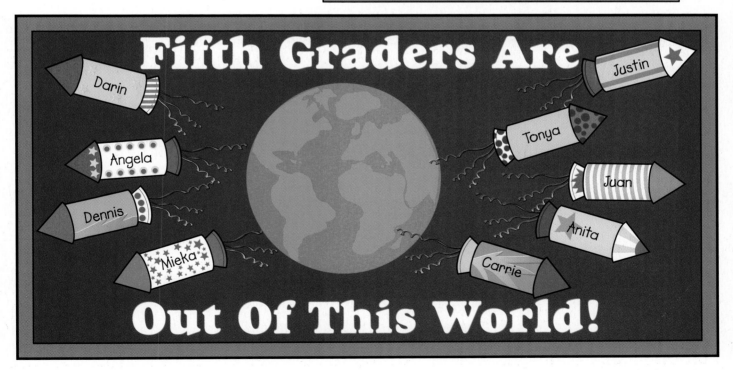

To prepare your new class for an out-of-this-world year, copy the **rocket pattern** (page 83) on white construction paper for each student. Have students personalize and decorate their rockets. Then direct each child to glue strands of red, yellow, and orange curling ribbon or tissue paper to the end of her rocket before posting it on a board as shown.

Diane Morgans—Gr. 5, Boswell Elementary, Lebanon, MO

Welcome parents to open house with this interactive back-to-school display. Copy a class supply of the **fish pattern** (page 84) on colorful construction paper. Have each student write his name on a fish and attach it to the board. Extend pieces of white yarn from the fishes to the top of the board. Add a small **hook pattern** (page 84) to the end of each line. During open house, invite parents to write messages to their children on the background paper.

Sharon Zacharda—Gr. 4, West View Elementary, Pittsburgh, PA

This welcome-back bulletin board is picture-perfect! Photograph each student holding a book while sitting in a chair. Make sure that each photo shows a side view of the student and that she faces the camera. Trim each photo, leaving only the student's image. Next, duplicate the **desk pattern** (page 85) on brown construction paper. Mount the patterns on black construction paper squares bordered with yellow to resemble chalkboards. To complete the display, add a student photo cutout to each desk.

Susan Patee—Gr. 5, Hillside Elementary, Farmington Hills, MI

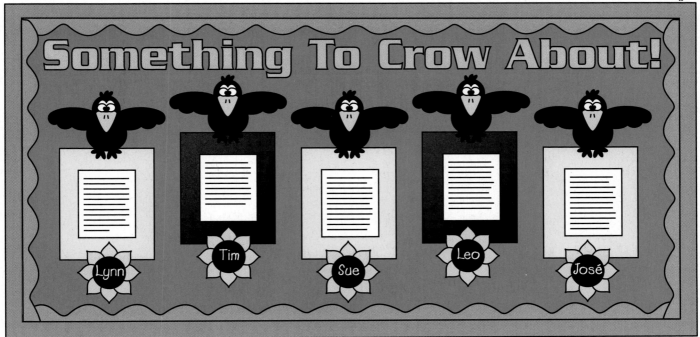

Recognize good work this fall with a display that's definitely something to crow about! Make several copies of the **crow pattern** (page 85). Color the beak of each crow yellow; then cut out the crows and mount them with construction paper as shown. Provide each child with art supplies to make a colorful sunflower labeled with her name. Each week post several papers and student sunflowers on the display as shown.

Colleen Dabney—Grs. 6–7, Williamsburg Christian Academy, Williamsburg, VA

For a book report project that's a treat to complete, make a class supply of the **candy corn pattern** (page 86). Have each student trace his pattern onto orange, yellow, and white paper as directed. Then have him cut out the tracings and label them with the information indicated on the templates. Finally, have the student glue his cutouts together on a piece of construction paper and cut out the completed piece of candy. Post the candy corn pieces on a bulletin board along with a trick-or-treat bag.

Brenda A. Keller—Gr. 5, Canadochly Elementary, East Prospect, PA

Count on reinforcing the importance of Halloween safety with this eye-catching display. Enlarge the **Halloween character pattern** (page 87) for several students to color. Have each student create a mock treat bucket from orange and black paper. Then have him use a fine-tip black marker to write a safety tip (such as "Get parents to inspect candy before you eat it") on the bucket. Display the buckets as shown.

Follow up a lesson on feelings—what causes them and how they are expressed on our faces—with this October display. Each student draws a caricature of a feeling discussed (see the list below) on a **pumpkin pattern** (page 88). Feature your patch of portraits on a colorful fall bulletin board as shown.

Lynn Marie Gilbertson—Gr. 4
James Sales Elementary
Tacoma, WA

exhausted	enraged
confused	ashamed
ecstatic	cautious
guilty	smug
suspicious	depressed
angry	overwhelmed
hysterical	hopeful
frustrated	lonely
sad	lovestruck
confident	jealous
embarrassed	bored
happy	surprised
mischievous	anxious
disgusted	shocked
frightened	shy

Celebrate diversity this October with this student-made display. After a discussion of the term *diversity,* have each student make his own unique jack-o'-lantern from construction paper to display on a bulletin board as shown.

Perry Stio, M. L. King School, Piscataway, NJ

This easy-to-make management tool doubles as a spooky seasonal display! Enlarge the **tombstone pattern** (page 89); then duplicate it onto gray construction paper (one copy for each classroom job). Enlarge the **ghost pattern** (page 90); then copy it onto white paper. Laminate and cut out the patterns. Program the tombstones and ghosts with a wipe-off marker. Rotate your haunted helpers daily by wiping the ghosts clean and then relabeling them.

What pet peeve drives you batty? Have students interview family members and friends to find out their pet peeves. Give each student a **bat pattern** (page 91) to trace on black paper. Then have him cut out the bat and embellish it with paper eyes and fangs. Instruct the student to cut out one white and one black cloud from paper; then have him describe a pet peeve on the white cloud. Arrange the bat and cloud shapes on a board as shown.

Julia Alarie—Gr. 6, Essex Middle School, Essex, VT

Team up with your students' families this Thanksgiving to create a display that shows a lot of heart! Have each student label a red, orange, or yellow paper heart with a sentence describing something for which he's thankful. After posting the hearts flowing out of a giant cornucopia as shown, give each child several smaller heart cutouts to take home. Direct the student to have each family member label a heart with a thankful thought. Add these smaller hearts to the display as a border.

"Tie-mely" expressions of thanks are what this board is all about! Send a note home requesting donations of old ties. Have students work together to create the turkey, stuffing newspaper behind a piece of burlap, felt, or paper for the body. Add the **turkey head pattern** (page 91). Arrange the ties and display students' writings about thankfulness or Thanksgiving as shown.

Marilyn Davison—Grs. 4–5, River Oaks School, Monroe, LA

Gobble up this easy-to-make student display for Thanksgiving. Enlarge the **turkey pattern** (page 92). Have each child trace a feather template on construction paper and cut out the tracing. Then have her label the top third of the feather with a brief summary of a favorite book. Add the feathers to the display.

David M. Olson—Gr. 5, Montgomery-Lonsdale Middle School, Montgomery, MN

Sharpen skills with a November display that doubles as a learning center. Place seasonal skill sheets in large pockets stapled to the board. Enlarge the **turkey pattern** (page 93); then color it, cut it out, and staple it to the board. Write each child's name on a cutout feather and add it to the display. Each time a student completes an activity, let him place a sticker on his feather.

Christine Juozitis—Gr. 4, Thomas Jefferson School, Binghamton, NY

What would your students want if they could each wish for one thing—that is, one thing that would not directly benefit each of them? Have each student write her wish on a **wishbone pattern** (page 94). Then display the wishbones with a colorful **Pilgrim pattern** (page 95). If desired, send additional wishbones home for parents to complete; then add these cutouts to the display.

Suzanne Hammer—Gr. 5, Louisa-Muscatine Elementary, Letts, IA

Winter

Display students' writings on this winter wonderland. Staple three white circles to the board, stuffing them with tissue paper for a 3-D effect. Use twigs and other art materials to complete the snowman. Have each student cut a large circle from an 8" x 8" sheet of white tissue paper; then have her copy her winter poem or haiku onto the circle using a black felt-tip pen. Next, have the student glue three 9" x ½" strips of brightly colored paper to make an asterisk shape and glue the poem in the center of this shape. Staple these poetic snowflakes around the snowman.

Dale Lindberg—Gr. 5, Stone Scholastic Academy, Chicago, IL

These shovel flip books are a great way to brighten up a wintry day when teaching any lesson. Provide each student with three 9" x 12" sheets of construction paper: one gray and two white. Then have each student follow these steps:

1. Measure one-half inch from the bottom of each sheet's short side and mark a line.
2. Stack the three sheets as shown, lining them up along the pencil lines.
3. Holding their bottoms as shown, fold over all three sheets to the pencil line of the top sheet and crease.
4. Staple near the fold.
5. Add a brown 2" x 18" construction paper handle.

Adapt this display for any skill or subject area. Simply change the title and have students use different headings on the paper tabs of their shovels.

Cindy Campbell—Gr. 4
Boswell Elementary, Lebanon, MO

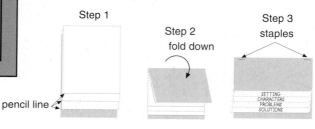

The weather outside may be frightful, but the reading incentive of this display is delightful! Make copies of the **snowflake book report form** (page 97). Have students cut out, color, and complete these forms when they want to recommend cool books they've read. Add a large copy of the **snowman pattern** (page 96) and small student-made snowflakes to the display for a wintry touch.

Gloria Twohig—Librarian, St. Matthew's School, Campbellsport, WI

To make this cheery holiday display, copy the **tree-light pattern** (page 97) on several different colors of construction paper. Have each student cut out a pattern and glue a photo of himself onto it. Mount the lights on a garland that has been attached to a board as shown.

A few days before students head home for the holidays, give each child his light and another light pattern that has been cut from tagboard. Have the student glue the colored light onto the tagboard pattern and write a message to his parents on the back. Laminate the lights; then punch a hole in the top of each one and insert an inexpensive key ring. How's that for turning a bulletin board into wonderful holiday gifts?

Jan Drehmel—Gr. 4
Korger Chestnut School
Chippewa Falls, WI

Spread the spirit of sharing with this shimmering display! Have students trace their hands on paper, cut out the tracings, and glue them to an enlarged copy of the **candle pattern** (page 98). Make a class supply of the candle and **holly leaf patterns** (page 98). Have each child label the center of his candle with a way he can brighten someone else's holiday season. Then have him glue tissue paper pieces and the cutout holly leaves onto his candle as shown.

Gerry McCue and David M. Olson—Gr. 5, Montgomery-Lonsdale Middle School, Montgomery, MN

Celebrate the holiday season with a down-home display! Have each student decorate a small paper sack to look like a house (either his own or one that reflects his interests in some way). After he stuffs the sack with newspaper and adds a paper roof, have him pin the house to a board decorated as shown. For a writing extension, have each child write a description of his house. Place the descriptions near the display. Then challenge students to match them to the correct homes.

Karen Riesterer—Gr. 6, Valders Middle School, Valders, WI

No time to make a holiday display? No problem! Mount large white letters, as shown, on a background of red foil paper. Ask students, "What is it about the holidays that makes you happy?" Let each child write his answer on a letter using a red or green felt pen. Have students add shiny gold and green self-sticking stars to the background for a simply dazzling display.

Deck the halls with a student-made display that sharpens research skills! Give each student an unlined index card. Have the student choose a country's flag to research; then have him illustrate the flag on his card. Arrange the flags in the shape of a holiday tree. Have students add shiny foil stars to the background for a finishing touch.

Julia Alarie—Gr. 6, Essex Middle School, Essex, VT

Celebrate your students' giftedness with this outstanding display. Make a class set of the **ornament patterns** (page 99). Have students decorate them with markers and glitter and hang them from a bulletin board tree. Provide each student with a cardboard rectangle to cover with holiday wrapping paper. Add a ribbon bow and a gift tag labeled with the student's name and her particular strength or "gift" (see below). Arrange the presents around the base of the tree.

William Turner—Gr. 5, Thaxton Elementary, Thaxton, VA

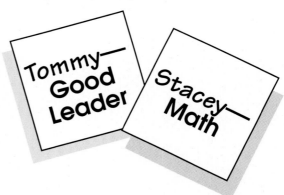

Make your classroom more cozy with a holiday display full of warm wishes. First, have each student create a construction paper quilt square similar to the examples shown. Then have him use paper, yarn, and bits of cloth to create a face that resembles his own. Arrange the quilt squares on a white background and add a scalloped dust ruffle across the bottom. Mount several of the faces in a row across the top. Replace the faces every few days until each student has displayed his creation.

Julie Alarie—Gr. 6, Essex Middle School, Essex, VT

Wrap up the year with a book report project that doubles as a holiday display! Duplicate a form similar to the one shown on 9" x 12" white construction paper. Then have each student follow these steps:

1. Fill out a form about your book.
2. Use tape or glue to cover a sheet of construction paper with holiday gift wrap.
3. Glue two construction paper strips as shown on the front of your gift-wrapped paper. Label the horizontal strip with your book's title.
4. Write the book's author and your name on a gift tag. Glue the tag to the gift-wrapped paper.
5. Staple the gift-wrapped paper atop your book report at the top only.

Post the reports on a board backed with bright foil paper. Encourage students to visit the display and lift the "package" atop each report to find out about their classmates' books. Add a wrapped box labeled as shown to remind students that a good book is one of the best gifts of all!

Brenda A. Keller—Gr. 5
Canadochly Elementary
East Prospect, PA

| Book: |
| Author: |
| Setting: |
| Characters: |
| Problem: |
| Review: |

Give yourself the gift of a good book!

Good work—how sweet it is! To display student papers during December, mount two candy canes on a board as shown. Make copies of the **gingerbread boy pattern** (page 100) on light brown paper. Have students cut out and color the patterns; then staple the patterns to the board along with paper candy cutouts. Copy the **candy paper topper** (page 100) on white construction paper. Give a topper to each student to cut out, color, and slip onto a favorite paper.

Michelle Fancher—Gr. 7, Immaculate Conception School, Indian Orchard, MA

Provide students with some sweet inspiration for creative writing with this hands-on display. Ask several students to draw and cut out pictures of their heads, wearing dreamy expressions. Mount these cutouts along the bottom of the board. Have another group of students draw and cut out a collection of sweet-tasting goodies, such as cookies, pies, cupcakes, etc. On the back of each goodie, write directions for a fun-filled activity, such as the following:

- List ten foods you think would be improved by adding chocolate chips.
- Name ten foods that contain the name of a place—like Boston cream pie.
- Make five rebus puzzles that contain the "pie" sound, such as python and pirate.
- Write a description of cotton candy for someone who has never seen it before.

Attach these "sugarplums" above the sleeping heads with pushpins. Invite each student to visit the board during free time, remove a sweet, and complete its activity.

Karoleigh K. Nitchman—Grs. 4–6
Hurtsboro School Foundation
Hurtsboro, AL

It's the Hanukkah season—a perfect time to promote teamwork with this bright display! Have students trace their hands on bright blue and white paper. After they cut out the tracings, have students outline the cutouts in glitter and arrange them to make a giant menorah as shown. Add cutout flames; then glow with pride at the shining results of your group effort!

Michelle Kasmiske—Gr. 4, Monroe Elementary, Janesville, WI

To ring in the New Year, enlarge the phone receiver shown and mount it on a board. Copy the **telephone pattern** (page 101) on light-colored construction paper for each student. Have the student complete the pattern, cut it out, and add it to the board. When you take down the display, keep the patterns. Then return them one morning in February so students can discuss the progress they've made on their goals.

Welcome the New Year with a goal-setting display that encourages students to shoot for the stars! On a door or bulletin board, display an enlarged copy of the **spaceship pattern** (page 102). Before the December holiday break, take a photo of each student; then cut out his figure from the developed picture and glue it onto a yellow posterboard star. Have each student glue his star to an index card labeled with a goal he'd like to shoot for in the New Year. Then collect the projects. When students return in January, have them review their stars and add them to the display. What a star-studded way to get students back on track after the holidays!

Nicole Heileson—Gr. 6
Samuel Morgan Elementary
Kaysville, UT

After discussing the goals Dr. Martin Luther King Jr. had for solving problems peacefully, have each student think of someone in his own life with whom he needs to make peace. Have the student write a peace treaty naming that person, explaining why he wants peace with him or her, and stating the terms of the peace. Instruct the student to copy his treaty onto a copy of the **dove pattern** (page 99); then have him trace and cut out another pattern from black paper. Staple each white dove over a black dove to create a shadow effect.

Kelly L. Simpson—Gr. 4, Newbury Elementary, Howell, NJ

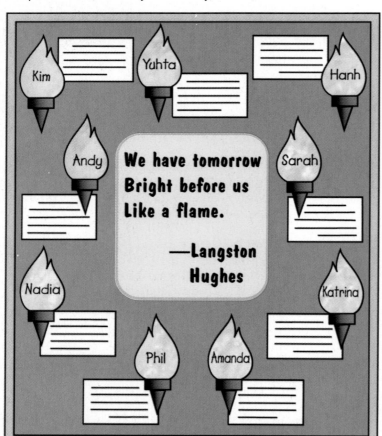

Spotlight Black History Month this February with the help of a famous Black American poet. Have each student cut out a flame shape from white construction paper. After coloring the flame with yellow and orange chalk, the student smudges the colors with a tissue and uses a black marker to label the flame with his name. Then he glues a small black rectangle and triangle to the flame as shown. Post the flames with the lines from Langston Hughes's poem "Youth" as shown. Finally, have each student add to the display a paragraph describing his burning desire for the future or explaining how tomorrow is like a flame.

Andrea Troisi
LaSalle Middle School
Niagara Falls, NY

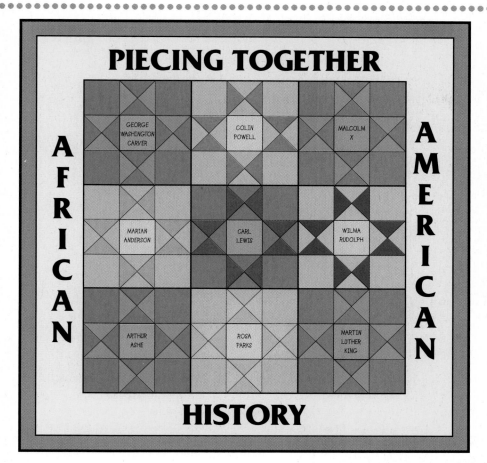

PIECING TOGETHER

A F R I C A N

GEORGE WASHINGTON CARVER

COLIN POWELL

MALCOLM X

MARIAN ANDERSON

CARL LEWIS

WILMA RUDOLPH

ARTHUR ASHE

ROSA PARKS

MARTIN LUTHER KING

A M E R I C A N

HISTORY

Piece together facts about famous African Americans during Black History Month with this eye-catching display. Make a class supply of the **quilt pattern** (page 103). Have each student write the name of a famous African American in the center square; then have him color the rest of the pattern. Mount the patterns to make a giant quilt. Choose one square from the quilt each morning during February; then have the student who researched that famous figure share facts about him or her.

Colleen Dabney—Gr. 5
Williamsburg Christian Academy
Williamsburg, VA

template placed slightly above fold

Hearty thanks are in full bloom with this February display! Staple a large paper basket on a bulletin board, leaving the rim unstapled. Near the display, place a heart template, scissors, tape, and a supply of long green pipe cleaners and construction paper. When a student wants to thank a classmate (or you!) for a kind deed, she traces the template on a folded sheet of paper (see above) and cuts out the tracing. Then she writes the kind person's name on the resulting card's front and a thank-you message inside. After taping the card to a pipe cleaner, she slips it into the basket. On Valentine's Day, let each person pluck her thank-yous from the basket. (Be sure a card is made for each student so that no one is left out.) For a variation, have each student write her note to the author of the book she's reading, saying thanks for a favorite scene or character.

Need a display that "heart-ly" takes any time to make? Staple an envelope cutout to a board as shown to hold seasonal activities. Give each student a heart cutout labeled with his name. Have him decorate his heart at home with family members. Mount finished hearts on doilies. Encourage students to fill their waiting time before Valentine's Day by completing an activity from the board.

David M. Olson—Gr. 5, Montgomery-Lonsdale Middle School, Montgomery, MN

Pour on the Valentine's Day spirit with this heartfelt display! Staple an enlarged copy of the **heart character pattern** (page 104) on the board. Copy the **heart patterns** (page 104) onto pink paper (one heart per child). Have each student choose a favorite assignment and staple it onto red construction paper; then have her fill out her heart pattern with reasons for her choice. Display the hearts with your students' papers.

Lisa LeFiles, Eastbrook Elementary, Winter Park, FL

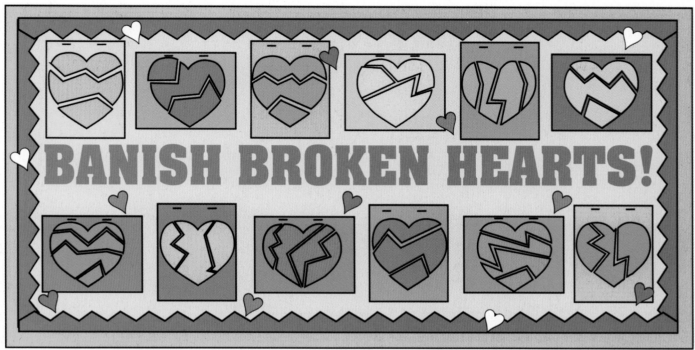

Have each student lightly draw two or more horizontal, diagonal, or vertical zigzag lines on a cutout heart. After cutting along the lines, the student glues the pieces as shown on a contrasting color of paper. As a class, brainstorm conflicts that often arise between friends, family members, classmates, etc. Have each student write a solution to one of the problems on another sheet of paper. Place each child's heart project atop his solution; then staple the two papers at the top and mount them on the board.

Jackie M. Matthys—Gr. 4, Jackson-Keller Elementary, San Antonio, TX

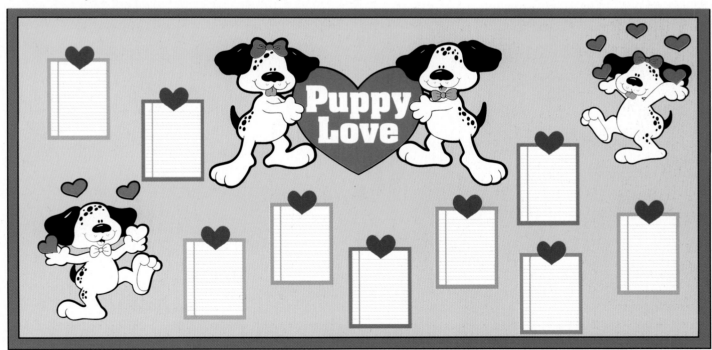

Get ready for Valentine's Day with puppies that love students' good work. Cover your board with pink or white background paper. Enlarge, color, and cut out the **puppies and hearts patterns** (pages 105 and 106). Have students cut out and decorate red hearts with lace, ribbon, markers, and glitter to accent papers.

Jackie M. Matthys—Gr. 4

Hearts Full Of Adjectives!

Amiable
Notable
Generous
Erudite
Lovable

For a Valentine's Day display that doubles as a vocabulary builder, have each student use a red marker to write her name vertically on a large pink heart shape. Then have her search in a thesaurus or dictionary for appropriate adjectives to fit each letter. As each child shares her heart with the class, have her explain the meanings of any new vocabulary words she used. Mount the hearts on heart-shaped doilies; then display them with the **character pattern** (page 107) as shown.

Marilyn Davison—Grs. 4–5, River Oaks School, Monroe, LA

"Plaid" About You!

For a bright Valentine's Day display, have each student create her own heart-shaped tartan. Explain to students that a *tartan* is a plaid pattern consisting of stripes of various widths and colors. The stripes cross at right angles against a solid background. Have each student fill a sheet of white construction paper with his tartan, using colored pencils, crayons, or markers; then have his cut a heart shape from the paper. Ask each student to write a paragraph about someone he is mad about. Post the paragraphs among the hearts.

Lisa Borgo—Gr. 4, East Hanover, NJ

Spring

For a St. Pat's display, copy the **shamrock pattern** (page 108) on green paper for each student. Have each student write about a time when she was lucky—without revealing her identity—on her shamrock. Then have her write her name lightly in pencil on the back of the cutout. Number the cutouts; then pin them to the board. Challenge students to guess the identity of each lucky person. Increase the mystery by adding shamrocks completed by staff members too!

Caroline Chapman, Vineland, NJ

Even non-Irish eyes are sure to smile at this nifty science display! In March provide time for students to research the human eye. Then have each child label a **shamrock pattern** (page 108) with a fact about the eye. Post the cutouts with photos of your smiling students as shown. Vary this idea by having students find facts about Ireland or any of the human body's five senses.

Melissa A. McMullen—Gr. 5, Saint Patrick School, Newry, PA

Mount a label for each cooperative team as shown. Copy the **book report form** (page 109); then place copies in a pocket attached to an enlarged **pot of gold pattern** (page 109). Each time a team member completes one of the book report forms, staple a $1 bill of play money above his team's label. (If the resulting bar graph begins to creep too high up the board, replace each set of $1 bills with a $5 bill.) The challenge to add another greenback to the board will spur students on to READ!

Marge McClintock—Gr. 5, Allen W. Roberts School, New Providence, NJ

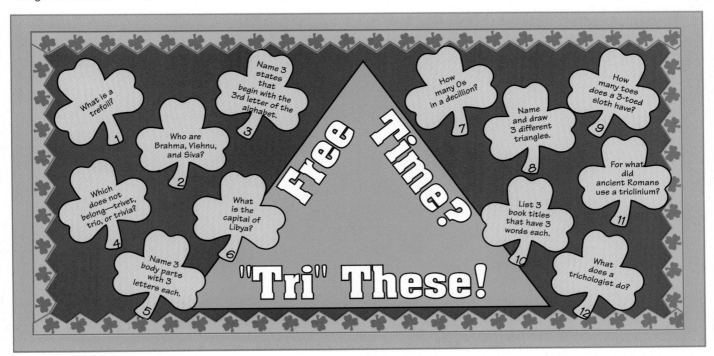

Everyone knows that Ireland's national symbol, the shamrock, is a small three-leafed plant, right? But what about other mysteries related to the number 3? Program **shamrock patterns** (page 108) with the research activities as shown. Have students work in groups of three and write their responses on large index cards. May the luck of the Irish be with them!

Invite ants to your classroom for a best behavior picnic! Cover a bulletin board with a paper picnic tablecloth. Attach paper plates, food cutouts, plasticware, napkins, and recycled juice boxes to the board as shown. For each day that the students exhibit good behavior, add one copy of the **ant pattern** (page 110) to the board. Once 20 ants have taken over the picnic, it's time to go out to lunch! Order pizza for the class or make other special lunch arrangements.

Colleen Dabney, Williamsburg Christian Academy, Williamsburg, VA

If tracking classroom job assignments keeps you hopping, try this easy helpers display. Copy the **frog pattern** (page 110) on brightly colored paper for each student. Have the student cut out his frog and label it with his name. Label a cutout lily pad for each classroom job; then mount the pads on the board. Assign jobs by simply pinning students' frogs on the lily pads.

Anita Miller—Gr. 4
Gage Elementary
Topeka, KS

Here's a bulletin board that will brighten any room during April's rainy days! Enlarge, color, and cut out the **umbrella pattern** (page 111); then staple it on the board and add a brown paper handle. Copy the **flower pattern** (page 111) on white paper. Have students color and cut out their flowers; then staple them as a border on the board. Finally, have students label large cutout raindrops with haiku or sentences about rain. Pin the raindrops to the board.

For a bright spring display, copy a **caterpillar pattern** (page 112) on green construction paper for each student. Label each pattern with an improper fraction; then distribute the caterpillars to students. Challenge each child to use construction paper scraps and other art materials to create a beautiful butterfly labeled with a mixed numeral to match his caterpillar's improper fraction. Post each caterpillar and butterfly on a spring bulletin board. If desired, have students add a border of paper flowers for a floral finishing touch.

Bethany Patterson—Gr. 6, Mount Airy, NC

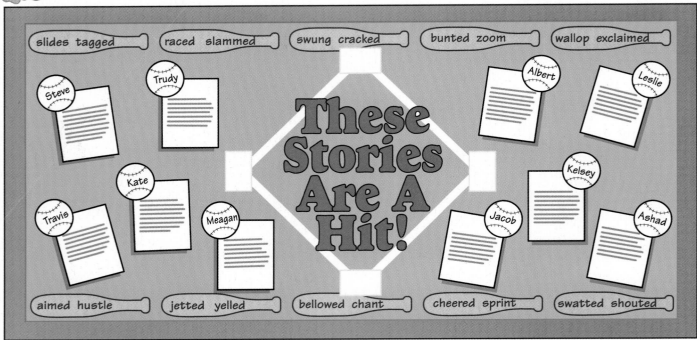

Celebrate America's love of baseball with this student-made display. Use masking tape to outline a baseball diamond on background paper. Add index cards for bases. Next, brainstorm with students a list of action verbs associated with baseball. Have each child write a baseball story that includes lots of vivid verbs (each underlined); then have her list some of her action verbs on a **baseball bat pattern** (page 112). Use the bats as a border for the board. Have each student write her name on a cut-out **baseball pattern** (page 112) to post with her story.

Nancy Rafay, Bartlett, TX

I could spend the day reading one of my favorite books, Charlie and the Chocolate Factory, and eating lots of chocolate!

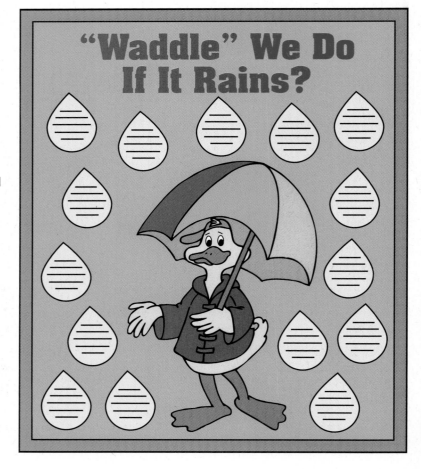

"Waddle" We Do If It Rains?

"Waddle" you do if you need a spring bulletin board or door display? Try this one! Post an enlarged copy of the **duck pattern** (page 113) on your classroom door or a bulletin board. Have each student add a large raindrop cutout that he's labeled with a paragraph describing how he could spend a really rainy day.

To practice critical thinking, adapt the title to "'Waddle' I Do If…" Under the title, post a sentence strip labeled with a challenging situation, such as "I forget my homework pad" or "My best friend hurts my feelings." Have each student write his response to the situation on a raindrop. Change the sentence strip each week.

Cyndi Smith—Gr. 6
Fairview Elementary
Carthage, MO

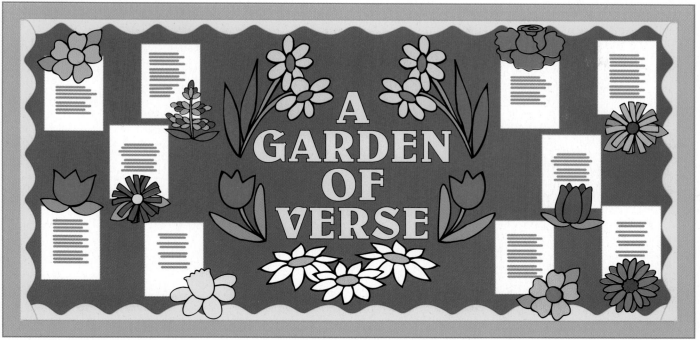

Cultivate a love of poetry with this easy-to-make display. Have each student cut out a large flower from a discontinued wallpaper book. Post each child's flower with a sample of his original poetry. Mount additional flowers around the title to complete your garden of glorious verses!

Colleen Dabney—Gr. 6, Williamsburg Christian Academy, Williamsburg, VA

Looking for a "bee-utiful" way to encourage good character? Write qualities of good character on enlarged **bee patterns** (page 114). Post the bees as shown. Place a basket of white **flower patterns** (page 114) near the board. Each time a student exhibits one of the qualities, have her write her name on a flower, color it, and staple the blossom to the board.

Colleen Dabney—Grs. 6–7, Williamsburg Christian Academy, Williamsburg, VA

To grow great grammar skills, have each student draw a large petaled flower on art paper. While students work, label a class supply of paper slips with concepts such as "adjectives," "plurals," and "suffixes." Then have each child select a slip, write its term and definition in his flower's center, and list examples on the petals. After students cut out and lightly color their flowers, post the blooms along with paper stems and leaves on the board.

Patty Smith—Gr. 5 Language Arts, Collins Middle School, Collins, MS

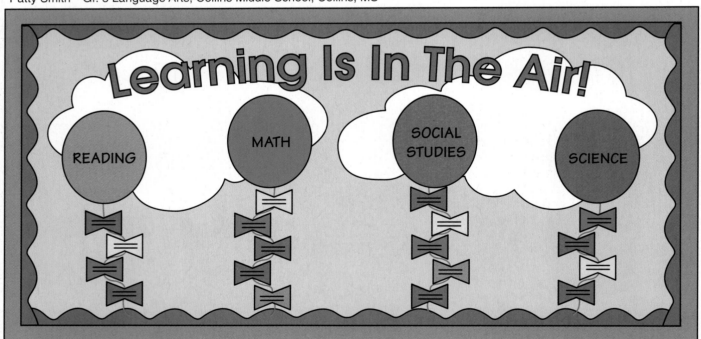

Help students find real-life applications for what they've learned with this high-flyin' idea! Display four balloon cutouts as shown. Tape a length of yarn to each cutout. When a student comes across a newspaper or magazine article, a television news report, or another item related to a topic recently studied (for example, a vocabulary word or a mixed numeral), have him describe the item on a small cut-out bow. Then have him tape the bow to the appropriate balloon's string.

Miriam Krauss—Grs. 4–5, Beth Jacob Day School, Brooklyn, NY

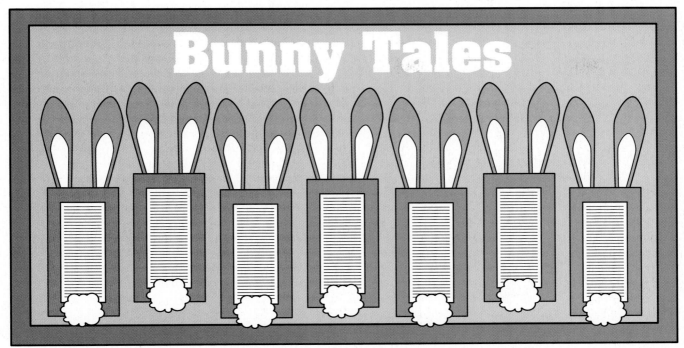

Bunny Tales

Look what's hopping down the bunny trail! Give each child two bunny ear patterns cut from white and pink construction paper. Have students glue the patterns together to make ears as shown. Mount copies of students' original Easter stories on pink rectangles, stapling two ears to the top of each rectangle. For a finishing touch, glue a fluffy cotton tail at the bottom of each story.

With this fun display, everyone will be eager to "pitch in" to keep your classroom running smoothly. For each classroom job, copy the **baseball glove pattern** (page 115) on brown construction paper. Cut out the gloves and label them with jobs. Copy the **baseball pattern** (page 115) on white paper for each student. Cut out the baseballs and label them with students' names. For an interesting border, mount baseball cards around the edges of the board.

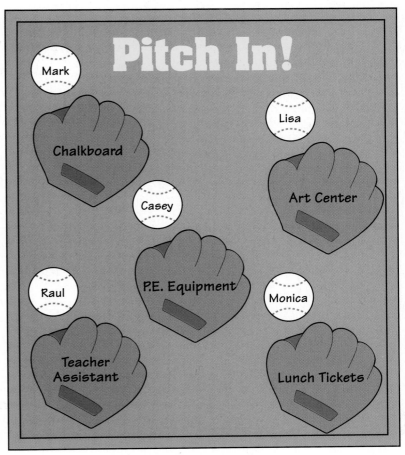

Celebrate Earth Day with a display that challenges everyone to pamper our planet. Paint a large earth on butcher paper and cut it out; then add facial features and several real bandages as shown. Have each student trace and cut out a bandage pattern from manila paper. Have the student label the cutout with her ideas for healing the earth's environmental woes. Mount the cutouts around the globe for a thought-provoking display.

Karen Krumanocker—Gr. 5
Rockland Elementary
Fleetwood, PA

Fines for all kinds of littering should be raised immediately! Maria

Celebrate a year that suited everyone to a "tee" with this easy-to-make door display! From a large folded sheet of white bulletin board paper, cut a T-shirt shape as shown above. After posting the shirt on the door, place a container of colorful markers nearby so students can autograph the shirt with their favorite memories of the year. Use this idea at other times of the year to celebrate a great book the class has just read, a field trip, or the birthday of a student or staff member.

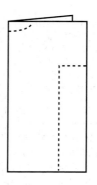

This Year Was "Tee-rrific"

because

I loved our field trip to the science museum! Kiara

Putting on the Christmas play was fun. Boyd

Learning Spanish was really cool! Simon

I made lots of new friends this year. Kim

My favorite subject was math. Leann

I liked our Thanksgiving service project. Devon

Ms. Anders told great jokes. Maddie

The computer lab was the place to be! Clay

EVERYTHING was great except homework. Lisa

Top off a "seed-sational" year with this juicy display! First treat students to a snack of fresh watermelon. Save and rinse the seeds. Then have each student complete the steps below to create a 3-D watermelon slice. Add a **watermelon pattern** (page 116), including vine and leaves, for a finishing touch. If desired, use the projects on a back-to-school bulletin board titled "It's Going to Be a 'Seed-sational' Year!"

Steps:

1. Trace a large circle on green tagboard. Cut out the tracing.
2. Trace a slightly smaller circle on pink tagboard. Cut out the tracing.
3. Use sponges and different colors of green paint to sponge-paint stripes on the green circle. Let dry.
4. Use sponges and red paint to sponge-paint the pink tagboard. Let dry.
5. Glue the pink circle atop the green one.
6. Glue watermelon seeds atop the pink circle.

Deborah Mayo—Gr. 5
Nebo Elementary
Jena, LA

Reflect on a super year with this sunny display! Copy a class supply of the **sunglasses pattern** (page 117) on construction paper. Have each student cut out his pattern and label its frames with favorite school year memories. Then have him stick a white file-folder label (cut in half) to the left lens and label it with his name. On the right lens, have him tape a small drawing of himself. Use the display again in August with the title "Reflections of Last Year's Class."

Traci Baker—Gr. 4, Brassfield Elementary, Bixby, OK

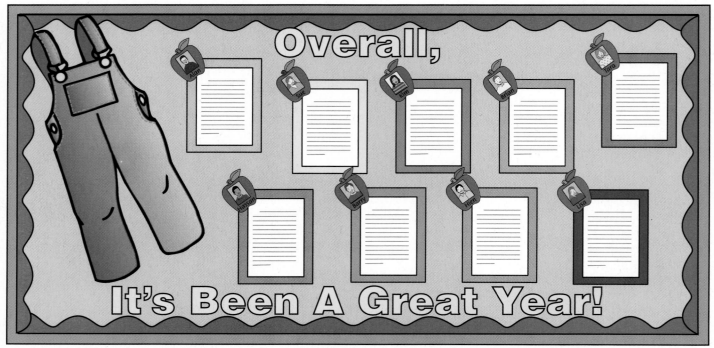

Highlight essays of the school year's most memorable moments with this eye-catching board. Pin a pair of child's overalls to the board. Then have each student color a copy of the **apple pattern** (page 83), cut it out, and tape a photo of herself on the cutout. Position each child's apple at the corner of her essay.

Tammy D. Taylor—Gr. 6, Franklin Elementary, Mt. Airy, NC

"Orange" you glad this end-of-the-year display is so simple to make? On an orange circle, have each student write a poem telling why one particular event, project, or activity made the year so much fun. Then display the circles with an enlarged **orange pattern** (page 118) as shown. Or combine students' poems—each written on a purple grape cutout—into a bunch on a board titled "Fifth Grade Was a Bunch of Fun!"

Theresa Hickey—Gr. 4, St. Ignatius School, Mobile, AL

Round out the school year with a rollicking year-end review! Give each student construction paper, scissors, markers, and glue for creating any type of ball—a basketball, a playground ball, etc. Next, have him write a question that reviews a concept he's learned during the year on the front of his ball and its answer on the flip side. Pin the balls to the board. Read one ball each day during the final weeks of school, challenging students to give the correct answer.

For an end-of-the-year display that's a flock of fun to make, have each of several groups make a birdhouse from a paper grocery bag. Mount the houses as shown. On the display, have each student add a **bird pattern** (page 118) labeled with a sentence describing her favorite activity of the year. At the start of next year, post the houses and birds again with the title "Fifth Grade's Going to Be a Flock of Fun!"

Colleen Dabney—Grs. 6–7
Williamsburg Christian Academy
Williamsburg, VA

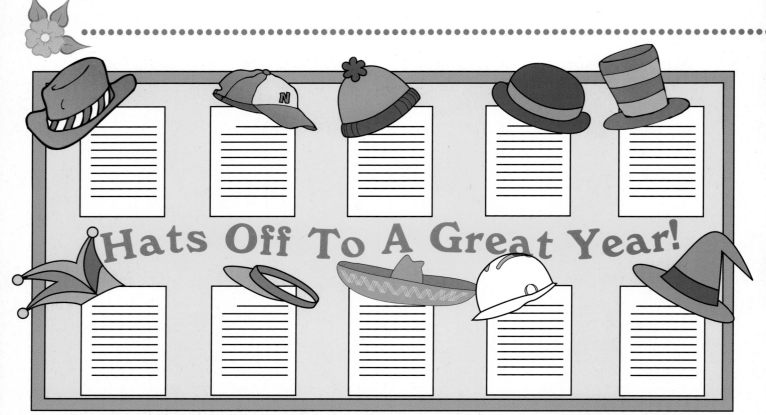

Cap off a great year by asking each student to bring a favorite or an unusual hat to school. As students wear their hats, have each one write a recap of the year's favorite events. Then have each student make a construction paper copy of her hat to put on the board atop her written recap.

Terry Healy—Gifted K–6, Eugene Field Elementary, Manhattan, KS

"Plant" a field of memories as your students prepare to move up to the next grade level. Cut 15–20 circles from brown construction paper. Cut a hole in each; then glue a photo of a class activity behind the hole. Have students glue yellow paper triangles around the edge of each frame. (For a 3-D effect, curl each resulting petal around a pencil.) If desired, glue several sunflower seeds on each brown frame. Mount the flower-framed photos onto the board, adding green paper stems and leaves.

Adapted from an idea by Karen Bryant, Rosa Taylor Elementary, Macon, GA

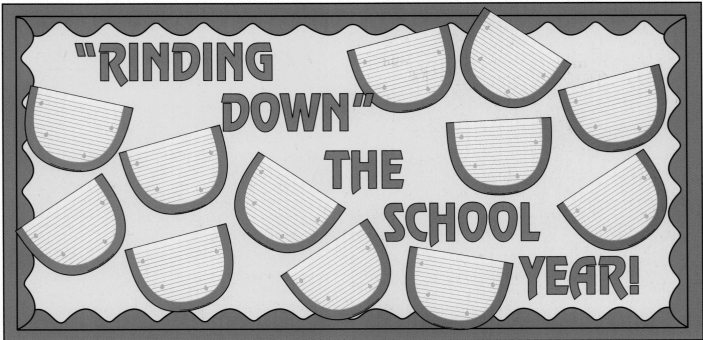

As the school year "rinds" down, take a moment to recall the fun times your class has shared. Have each student create a short poem chronicling a memorable school-year activity. Make a class set of the **watermelon pattern** (page 119) on pink paper. After each student has written his poem on a pattern, have him color the rind green and cut out the pattern. Let students glue real watermelon seeds onto the papers for a 3-D effect. Share the poems while enjoying a snack of watermelon.

Theresa Hickey—Gr. 4, St. Ignatius School, Mobile, AL

Say goodbye to the school year with this simple display. Cover a bulletin board with paper. Add the title "We're Signing Off!" and the **sign painter pattern** (page 120). Have each student record his most memorable moment directly on the board. As students enjoy the freedom of "writing on the board," you'll gain insight into the school-year events that left an impact.

Julie Plowman—Gr. 6, Adair-Casey Elementary, Adair, IA

Let the fun shine with this sunshiny poetry display! Purchase a class supply of bright yellow picnic plates (or spray-paint white paper ones). Have each child trace around her hands several times on yellow paper; then have her cut out the tracings and glue them around the rim of a plate to create a sun. Finally have her write a poem about having fun in the springtime sun and glue it in the center of the plate. Better grab those sunglasses!

Heidi Graves—Gr. 4
Wateree Elementary
Lugoff, SC

Want your students to go bananas over books this summer? Ask your media specialist for a grade level–appropriate list of good books to recommend for summer reading. Enlarge, color, and cut out the **monkey head and feet patterns** (page 121). Make a large tagboard book labeled with the title and poem as shown. Glue two cut-out hands and a pocket in which to hold the reading lists to the book; then mount it with the monkey patterns on a bulletin board. Encourage each student to grab a list and get started on some super summer reading!

Ann Nicklawske McGee—Gr. 4
Oakdale Elementary
Oakdale, MN

Are you having trouble?
Are you singing the blues
Because you don't know
Which books to choose?
Don't be in despair!
Just look and you'll see!
Here's a list of great books
Recommended by me!

A Guide To Great Books

Anytime

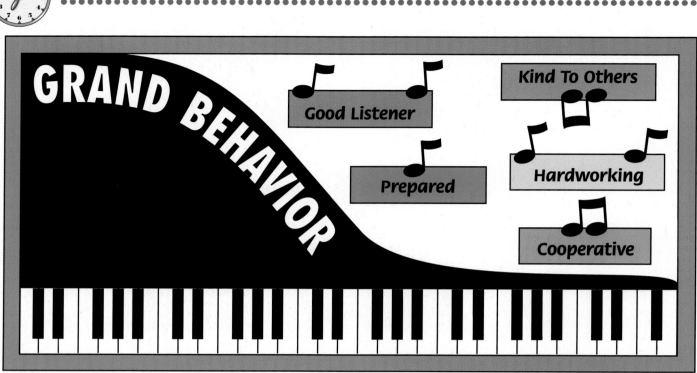

Good behavior is music to any teacher's ears! Decorate a board as shown to resemble a grand piano. Ask your class, "What makes a good student?" List their responses on the board; then have students select the top five. Write these noteworthy qualities on tagboard strips to mount on the board with cutout notes. Use this idea to display "Grand Work," "Grand Writing," or other student projects.

Colleen Dabney—Grs. 6–7, Williamsburg Christian Academy, Williamsburg, VA

For a "hand-y" way to encourage good character, have student volunteers color a large cutout globe and staple it to a board as shown. Next, ask each child to trace her hand five times on colorful paper and cut out the tracings. Collect the cutouts in a shoebox labeled "Helping Hands." Each time you witness a student helping someone else, describe the kind act to the class and staple a cutout along the globe's edge. When the entire globe has been encircled, celebrate by holding a Helping Hands Hoedown. Then remove the hand cutouts and start the challenge again!

Beverly Langland—Gr. 5
Trinity Christian Academy
Jacksonville, FL

It never fails. No matter how well you plan, there's always at least one student who finishes early and says, "What do I do now?" Solve this dilemma with a simple display. Enlarge, color, cut out, and post the **clock pattern** (page 122). Beside the cutout, post a laminated piece of poster board. On the poster, use a wipe-off marker to list activities that students can do in their free time. Wipe it clean when you want to change the list.

Some Extra Time?

Try these!

1. Bulletin board activities

2. Journal

3. Math incentives

4. Folders

5. Basic skills packets

6. Read library book

7. Vocabulary

8. Read today's newspaper

Get It Together This Year
By Using

T	E	A	M	W	O	R	K
Trying your best.	Each person accepting responsibility.	Always staying on task.	Managing your time.	Willingness to cooperate.	Organizing your time and work.	Reaching the goals set.	Keeping the noise level low.

This classroom display encourages teamwork! Make eight copies of the **body pattern** (page 123). Write a letter from the word *teamwork* on each pattern; then cut out the patterns and distribute one to each of eight groups. Have each group create a cutout head, tape it to the pattern, and then color the pattern. Display the projects as shown. Add steps for accomplishing teamwork—each beginning with one of the word's letters—as handy reminders.

Introduce students to their new class's rules with this "tasteful" display! Enlarge, color, and cut out the **chef pattern** (page 124). Write your class rules on the chef's apron. Coming out of a large black pot, staple colorful index cards labeled with the privileges students will enjoy when they follow class rules. To adapt this board to a "Cookin' Up Good Writing!" learning center, write the center's directions on the chef's apron and student writing tasks on the index cards.

Sherra Sterling
Colonial Hills Elementary
Houston, TX

Motivate good work habits with this hot-diggity display! Post an enlarged copy of the **dog pattern** (page 124) as shown. Have students help you cut out 101 spots from white paper. Whenever you spot a child working hard, staple a cutout to the board and number it. When the class earns 101 spots, celebrate with cookies-and-cream ice cream or Oreo cookies.

adapted from an idea by Hunter Burrow—Gr. 4, South Salem Elementary, Salem, VA

If students are motivated to do their best, chalk it up to this easy display! First, prepare a supply of seasonal cutouts, such as mittens for January, hearts for February, etc. Cover a bulletin board with black paper. Then let students use white chalk to decorate the board with phrases that describe their best work. Each time a student receives an exemplary grade, let him write his name and grade on a cutout and add it to the display as shown. When there's no more room for cutouts, celebrate with a class party. Then prepare a new set of cutouts and start again!

Teresa DeWeese—Gr. 5
James Lewis Elementary
Blue Springs, MO

Promote a "can-do" attitude in your classroom! Direct each student to turn a 6" x 12" sheet of construction paper horizontally and decorate it as shown. Have the student roll his paper into a cylinder and tape the edges together; then have him trace the can's circumference onto paper to make a circle to tape to the bottom of his can. Staple the cans to the board. Place a supply of 1" x 8" paper strips nearby. Have students list each other's successes—such as "Aaron can draw cool pictures"—on the strips and drop them in their classmates' cans.

Karen Steinwachs, Chicago, IL

Hang On To Good Character!

honest

respectful

kind

responsible

helpful

good listener

confident

sympathetic

sense of humor

understanding

hardworking

patient

Motivate your class to consider the qualities of good character with this display. Pin two lengths of cord across a board. Have students brainstorm a list of positive character traits; then have each child write one trait on a clothing cutout to clip on the clotheslines. Each morning choose several traits for students to discuss and write about in their journals.

Beverly Langland, Trinity Christian Academy, Jacksonville, FL

"Udder-ly" Awesome!

Dion

For an "udder-ly" awesome self-esteem activity, enlarge the **cow pattern** (page 125) and post it on a small bulletin board. Have each student use a black marker to decorate a white paper bag with cow spots and his name. Add a label to an empty milk bottle (or a milk carton with the top cut off) that reads "Crème de la Crème." As you observe a student exhibiting exemplary behavior or study skills, have that child label a slip of paper with his name and drop it in the bottle. At the end of the day, draw one slip from the bottle. Post that student's bag on the board; then have classmates fill the bag with written "cow-pliments" about the honored child.

Linda Archibeque Trimberger—Gr. 4
Jackson Elementary
Greeley, CO

Motivate students to lend a hand with this colorful helpers display! On a small bulletin board, post library pockets labeled with your classroom jobs. Have each student trace one hand on a sheet of construction paper; then have him cut out the tracing and label it with his name. Assign jobs daily or weekly simply by inserting a hand cutout in each pocket. Decorate the board further with additional hand cutouts. Now isn't that a handy way to assign jobs?

Kathy Hillsman—Gr. 5
Douglas School
Danville, IL

Send the message that actions speak louder than words. Have each student draw a large flower outline on colorful paper. On an index card, have the student write a description of a good intention she has had and how she acted on it. Post the cards and flowers on the board with a copy of the **parrot pattern** (page 126). Add the title and large leaf cutouts as shown.

Mrs. Bednar, Mrs. Branagan, Miss Emery, and Mrs. Pace—Gr. 6, Sayreville Middle School, Sayreville, NJ

Set aside a spot to share everyone's good news with this idea! Label and display a six-inch paper circle for each student as shown. Encourage students to share their good news—awards, newspaper clippings, birth announcements, photos, etc.—by stapling them onto their spots. Periodically remove old spots and replace them with new ones.

Pat Twohey—Gr. 4, Old County Road School, Smithfield, RI

SMART COOKIE RECIPE

1 1/2 c. studying	2 3/4 c. effort
1 1/4 tsp. neatness	1/8 tsp. confidence
3/4 c. practice	1 good night's sleep

Mix together well. Then enjoy the great grade you've earned!

Cook up a batch of better work habits with this yummy display! Decorate a bulletin board with a plastic tablecloth and **cookie patterns** (page 127). Give each of several groups a giant poster board recipe card. On its card, have each group write a recipe that describes the study habits of a "smart cookie." On Monday post one of the group's recipes along with excellent student papers. At the end of the week, replace the card with another group's recipe.

adapted from an idea by Andrea Wohl—Gr. 5, Washington School, Westfield, NJ

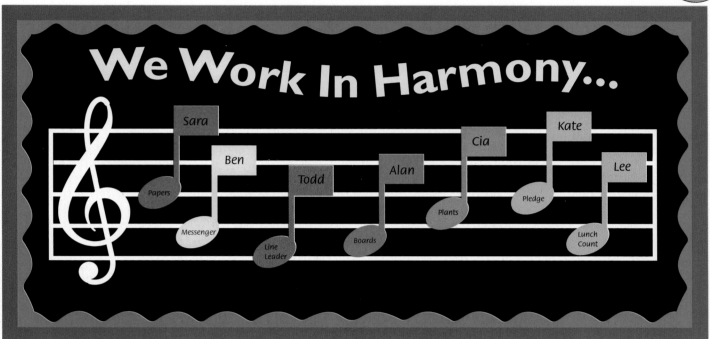

Harmonious helping abounds with this class helpers board! Use chalk to draw a music staff and clef sign on black background paper. Label a note cutout with each job. Laminate the notes; then assign jobs by writing students' names on them with a wipe-off marker. Each week allow new helpers to rearrange the notes' placement. A different melody will always be playing!

Rebecca R. Amsel—Gr. 4, Yeshiva Shaarei Tzion, Piscataway, NJ

Here's a group assignment display that doubles as a class photo gallery. Cut out one artist palette for each group. Label a construction paper circle for each student. To assign students to groups, place the circles on the palettes. To reassign groups, simply move the circles. Display photos of group activities on the board also.

Cathy Ogg—Gr. 4, Happy Valley Elementary, Johnson City, TN

Encourage teamwork with a nifty acronym and this cheery display! Draw slanting lines on a board as shown. Staple cutout pennants labeled with student names to the lines. Discuss the acronym TEAM (Together Everyone Achieves More!); then post the motto on the board. Each time a student successfully teams up with a classmate, have her describe the situation on an index card to post on the board.

Perry Stio, M. L. King School, Piscataway, NJ

Give everyone a "squeak" preview of the week ahead with this year-round display. Label five **cheese patterns** (page 128) with the days of the week; then laminate the patterns and post them with a large **mouse pattern** (page 128). Each week use a wipe-off marker to label the cheeses with special events, due dates, and reminders. On Friday simply wipe the display clean and reprogram it for the upcoming week.

Colleen Dabney—Grs. 6–7, Williamsburg Christian Academy, Williamsburg, VA

54

For this self-esteem display, enlarge the **take-out box pattern** (page 129). Have each student cut a fortune cookie from manila paper and label a white paper strip with his name. Collect the strips; then write a compliment on the back of each. Mount the cookies with the strips as shown. Adapt this for a terrific back-to-school display by writing welcome messages on the backs of the strips.

Colleen Dabney—Grs. 6–7, Williamsburg Christian Academy, Williamsburg, VA

Celebrate class birthdays with the help of a doggie that's long on fun! Copy the **head and tail patterns** (page 130) onto brown paper. Connect the head and tail with a long strip of brown paper labeled as shown. Have each student write his name and birthdate on a colorful card; then have students arrange the cards as shown to make a giant bar graph. Add balloons, confetti, and streamers for a display that's hot diggity done!

Perry Stio, M. L. King School, Piscataway, NJ

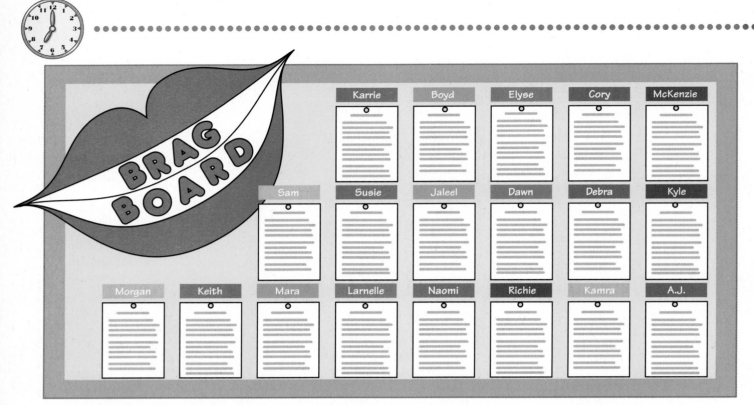

Looking for a display that stays up all year long? Here's one that will put a smile on your face! Post a nameplate for each student on a board decorated with a giant grin. Place a thumbtack under each nameplate. Then let each student post any paper she wants to brag about under her nameplate.

Shannon Hillis—Gr. 5, La Maddalena American School, Italy

Brush up self-esteem with this group good-work display! Post simple easel, paintbrush, and palette cutouts as shown. Each week display papers selected by members of one student group. Accent each paper with a cutout paint splotch labeled with the student's name. On Monday feature a different group's work on the display. Also use this idea to showcase honor roll students, your school's extracurricular activities, or other items of interest.

adapted from an idea by Libby Stanley and
   Dayna Sullivan
Browning Springs Middle School
Madisonville, KY

Shine the spotlight on great work! Laminate a yellow circle for each student. Cut a slit in each circle and attach two paper clips. Have each student use stencils to trace his name—connecting all letters—on tagboard. After coloring and cutting out his name, have the student staple it atop his circle. Periodically have each child select a paper to clip on his spotlight, along with a completed copy of the **assignment form** (page 131).

Bonnie Gibson—Gr. 5, Kyrene Monte Vista School, Tempe, AZ

This is "nacho" run-of-the-mill bulletin board! Add sizzle to your students' best work by copying the **red-pepper pattern** (page 131). Have a student volunteer color each pattern and cut it out. Display the peppers with papers your students have chosen to display. For a touch that's truly south of the border, back the bulletin board with a colorful piece of Mexican-style fabric.

Colleen Dabney—Grs. 6–7
Williamsburg Christian Academy
Williamsburg, VA

Looking for a colorful way to display your students' artwork? Enlarge the **bucket and brush patterns** (page 132) to color, cut out, and mount on a bulletin board. Cut free-form shapes from bright construction paper. Staple each cutout with a piece of artwork to create a display that's sure to make a splash with your class!

Colleen Dabney—Grs. 6–7, Williamsburg Christian Academy, Williamsburg, VA

Show off spotless papers with this adorable display. Enlarge the **dog pattern** (page 133). Attach it to the board and add a rolled-up newspaper near its mouth, labeled as shown. Duplicate one **pawprint pattern** (page 133) for each child. Write students' names on the patterns with white chalk or crayon. Then attach the prints to the bulletin board with good work. A "paws-itively" cute bulletin board!

Colleen Dabney, Williamsburg Christian Academy, Williamsburg, VA

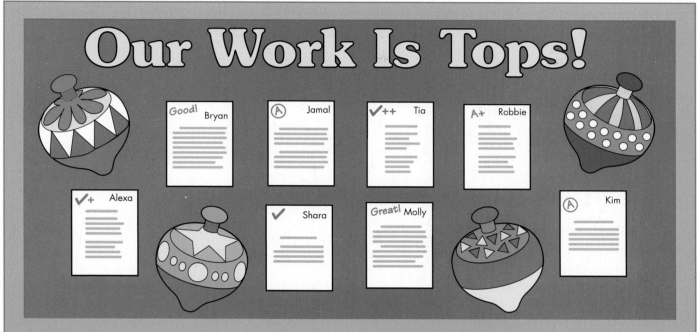

Highlight top-notch work with an easy student-made display! Have each student group decorate a copy of the **top pattern** (page 134) together. Post the tops on a bulletin board as shown. Each week ask one group's members to choose their favorite papers to post on the board. When you change groups, remove the tops and have teams decorate new ones for the display.

Colleen Dabney—Grs. 6–7, Williamsburg Christian Academy, Williamsburg, VA

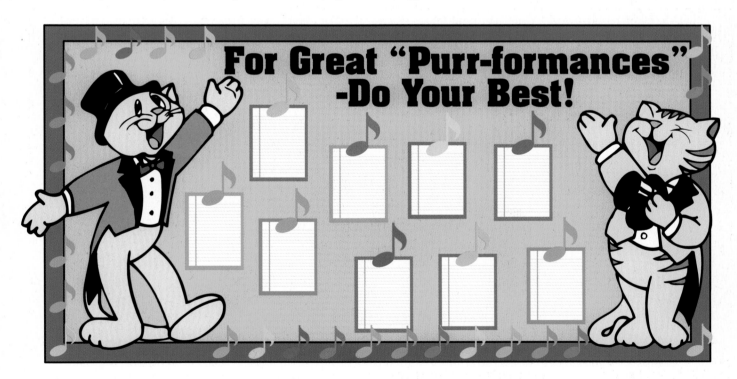

For great "purr-formances," encourage students to do their best! Cover your board with orange background paper. Enlarge, color, and cut out the **top-hat cats patterns** (pages 135 and 136). Have students make a border of colorful musical notes. Place a musical note above each child's paper.

Turn old jeans into a new "denim-ite" display with this idea! Pin a pair of jeans to a board. Have each child use construction paper scraps and glue to fashion a designer pair of pants and shoes as shown. Then have the student attach a favorite paper to the board and pin her cutout just below it. "Pants-tastic!"

Ina Dobkin—Gr. 5, East Elementary, Littleton, CO

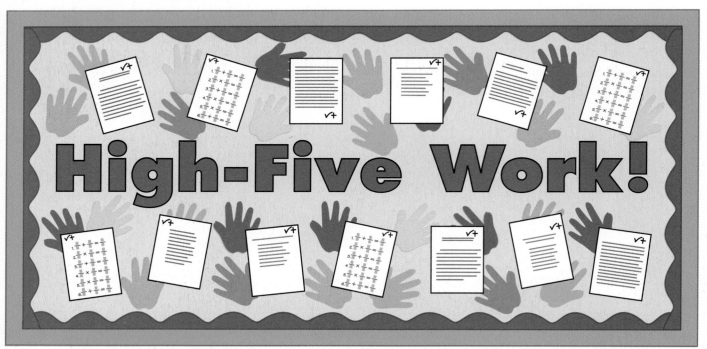

The best part of this good-work display is preparing the background paper! Cover a bulletin board with white (or any light-colored) paper. Pour several colors of fluorescent paints in pie pans. Have each student gently place his hand, palm down, in a pan of paint and then make a handprint on the bulletin board paper. When the paint has dried, use the board for highlighting students' outstanding work.

Shannon Berry—Gr. 4, Heritage Christian School, Brookfield, WI

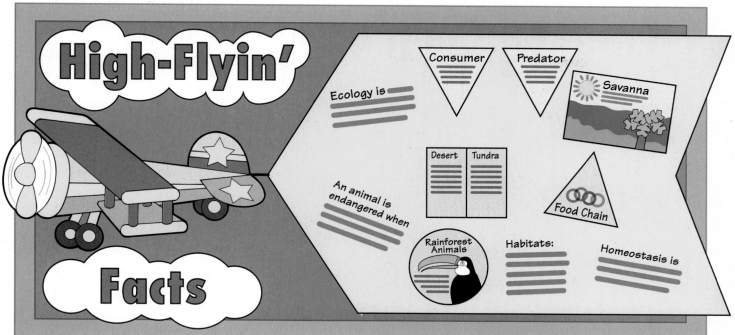

Review any topic with this high-flyin' display! Enlarge and color a copy of the **plane pattern** (page 137). Mount it on a board with a banner-shaped piece of bulletin board paper. At the end of a unit, have students decorate the banner with facts about the topic. Attach a new banner when you're ready to review the next unit.

adapted from an idea by Jeri Daugherity—Gr. 5, Mother Seton School, Emmitsburg, MD

Piece together an activity on writing personal essays with this colorful display! Have each child write an essay about a personal experience. After editing and proofreading, have the student rewrite her essay on a copy of the **puzzle pattern** (page 138). Then have her glue the essay onto a larger sheet of construction paper and trim the construction paper to make a $1/2$-inch border. Piece of cake!

Cynthia D. Davis—Gr. 6, Bonaire Middle School, Warner Robins, GA

Post a strip of white paper decorated to resemble a piano keyboard on a board as shown. Copy the **note pattern** (page 139) on colorful paper. Each morning introduce a new vocabulary word by giving students the first few letters of the word and letting them try to guess its identity. After the word has been guessed or revealed, discuss its meaning for students to copy in their vocabulary notebooks. Label a note cutout with the word, its part of speech, and the name of the student who correctly guessed the word. When the board is completely filled with notes, let student groups create quizzes to test classmates on the words.

Chava Shapiro, Monsey, NY

Fishin' for a way to hook your students on math? Give each child a copy of the **fish pattern** (page 140). Have him write a math problem on his fish with a fine-tipped black marker; then have him color and cut out his fish, and staple it on the board. Next, have each student write his problem's answer on a cutout bubble. Scatter the bubbles around the display; then challenge students to match each fish with its bubble.

Sora Miriam Zucker—Gr. 5, Beth Jacob Day School, Brooklyn, NY

Keep track of students' progress on writing projects with this fun display! Draw and label a simple gameboard on a paper-covered board as shown. Also copy, cut out, and label a game **pawn pattern** (page 140) for each student. As a child works on a writing piece, have her pin her pawn to the display to show where she is in the writing process. Point out to students that, just like in a board game, a writer may have to move her pawn back a few spaces as she works.

Kimberly Feldman—Gr. 6, Salt Brook Elementary, New Providence, NJ

If you're looking for a way to motivate reading, pop this board up in your classroom! Enlarge the **popcorn bucket pattern** (page 141) and mount it on a bulletin board. Make a class supply of the **popcorn pattern** (page 141) onto white paper. Have each student fill out his pattern with a brief review of a favorite book; then have him outline the pattern with a yellow marker before cutting it out and pinning it on the board. Use the same idea to make a "Good Work Is Popping Up All Over!" display.

Julie Eick Granchelli—Gr. 4, Towne Elementary, Medina, NY

Your students can bone up on science facts with this fun bulletin board. Enlarge the **dog pattern** (page 142). Copy the **bone pattern** (page 143) on white paper. Write science facts, review questions, or vocabulary words on the bones; then cut them out. Post patterns on a bulletin board as shown. Use this display to introduce a unit or as a review. Change the title and make more bones to adapt the display to other subject areas or skills.

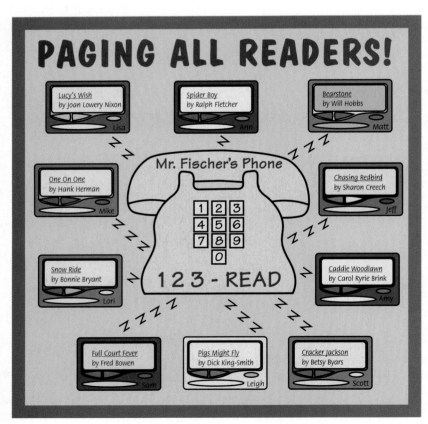

Alert students to prepare for book talks with this unique display. Modify the **telephone pattern** (page 101) as shown and mount it on the board. Use a black marker to draw the transmission lines. Give each child a **pager pattern** (page 143) to decorate with his name and the title and author of the book he's just read. Post several pagers on the board. Explain that students whose pagers have been posted have one week to prepare a brief book talk and a written summary. As students present their book talks, remove the pagers from the board, tape them to the tops of their summaries, and reposition them around the perimeter of the board. Change the pagers on the board each week until everyone has had a turn.

Rusty Fischer
Cocoa Beach, FL

Brush Up On Facts!

Encourage students to brush up on addition, subtraction, or multiplication facts or to find the answers to science or social studies research questions. Cover your board with yellow background paper. Enlarge, color, and cut out the **painter patterns** (page 144 and 145). Copy the **paintbrush** and **paint can patterns** (page 146). Program, color, and cut out the patterns. Have students match cans to brushes. Or write a question on each brush cutout and have students write the answers on the cans.

Drive up spelling scores with this traffic-stopping idea! Post an enlarged copy of the **traffic light pattern** (page 147). Make a class supply of the **traffic sign patterns** (page 146). Each time a student receives an excellent or improved grade on a spelling test, have him label a pattern with his name. Then have him color the sign and add it to the board.

Tamara Logan—Gr. 4
Heritage Christian School
Findlay, OH

Great Spelling Is a Go!

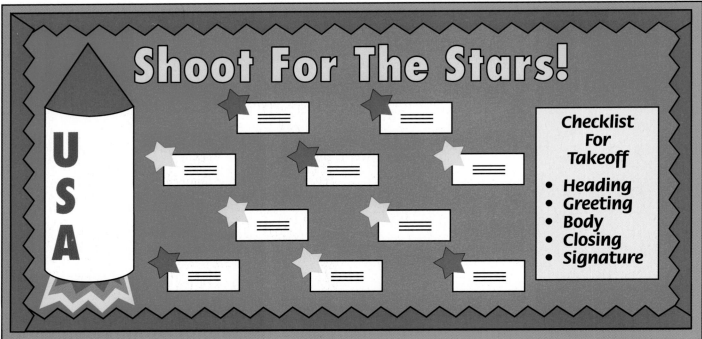

Help starstruck students sharpen their letter-writing skills with an out-of-this-world display! Post an enlarged **rocket pattern** (page 148) on a board. Ask your media specialist for reference books that list the addresses of popular entertainers, sports teams, and other famous folks. Select several addresses; then write each one on an envelope and post it, along with a **star pattern** (page 148), as shown. Encourage each student to choose an address and write a letter. If desired, provide stamped envelopes in which students can mail their letters.

Colleen Dabney—Grs. 6–7, Williamsburg Christian Academy, Williamsburg, VA

To make this striking display, enlarge the **pins** and **bowling ball patterns** (page 149). Mount them on a bulletin board as shown. Make multiple copies of the **bowling pin pattern** (page 149). When a student reads a book, have her write a brief review of it on a pin; then have her cut out the pin and staple it to the board. When a student has read and reviewed ten books, applaud her "reading strike" by giving her a pass to a local bowling alley.

Colleen Dabney—Gr. 5
Williamsburg Christian Academy
Williamsburg, VA

THESE BOOKS ARE RIGHT DOWN OUR ALLEY!

To serve up sizzling spelling practice, have each child cut out 20 eggs from white paper and label the top of each with a scrambled spelling word. Then have students swap eggs with partners and write the correct spelling on the bottom half of each egg. After swapping eggs again and checking each other's work, direct students to color a yolk on each correct egg before stapling it in the skillet or on a paper plate.

Jamie Drewry—Gr. 5, Wilson Elementary, Lawton, OK

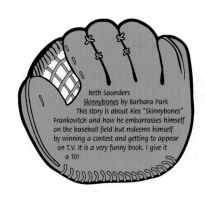

Beth Saunders
Skinnybones by Barbara Park
This story is about Alex "Skinnybones" Frankovitch and how he embarrasses himself on the baseball field but redeems himself by winning a contest and getting to appear on T.V. It is a very funny book. I give it a 10!

This student-created board is a real winner! After a student has read a sports book, have her draw a life-size outline of one item of sports equipment mentioned in the story. After cutting out the drawing, the student labels the cutout with her name, the book's title and author, a two- or three-sentence synopsis of the story, and a rating (1–10, with 10 being the best) of the book. Decorate a bulletin board to look like an open closet with shelves. Arrange the cutouts on the display as shown.

Julia Alarie—Gr. 6, Essex Middle School, Essex, VT

Encourage summer reading with this delightful deep-sea display! Enlarge, color, and cut out the **octopus pattern** (page 150), cutting slits where indicated. Have each student write a brief review of a favorite book on an index card. Place eight cards in the octopus's arms (changing them weekly). Have each student list her classmates' recommendations on a copy of the **book form** (page 150). Then add to the display students' drawings of scenes from the books.

Diane Hasler—Gr. 5, North Daviess Intermediate, Plainville, IN

Color this creative-writing display a "hue-ge" success! Challenge each student to write a paragraph that describes a new color he's invented and tells why it is needed. After the paragraphs are written, give each child an enlarged copy of the **crayon pattern** (page 151). Direct the student to label his pattern with the new color's name; then have him use colored pencils or crayons to color the pattern with his new color. Post the crayons in and around a crayon box pattern labeled with your name. Add the paragraphs for a finishing touch to this colorful display.

Michele Curlings—Gr. 6, Irmo Middle School, Columbia, SC

THE RIGHT COMBINATION

Lockers labeled: 1,050 | 1,981 | 345 | 5,436 | 2,317 | 1,054 | 3,252 | 3,320

Locks labeled: 210×5 | 283×7 | 115×3 | 604×9 | 331×7 | 527×2 | 813×4 | 664×5

For the right combination of fun and practice, cover a board with light blue paper. Use a black marker or tape to divide the paper into eight lockers. Copy the lock pattern (page 152). Label each lock with a math problem. Write each answer on a paper strip. Staple the strips to the lockers as shown; then challenge students to pin each lock to the correct locker. Provide an answer key. Change the locks and numbers frequently.

Colleen Dabney, Williamsburg Christian Academy, Williamsburg, VA

Country: _Argentina_
Expert: _Jessie_

If your students research individual countries, here's an interactive way to display their geographic know-how. Copy the **card cover pattern** (page 152) for each child to color. Cut sheets of construction paper in half lengthwise; then give one half-sheet to each student to fold in half again to make a card. Have the student glue his pattern to the front of his card and write a question about his country on the inside. Post the cards around a world map, attaching each to its matching country with yarn. During free time, a student can try to answer a classmate's question from the board. The student checks his answer with the "expert" who's studying that country.

Michelle Bachler—Grs. 5–6
Meadow Elementary
Lehi, UT

Tip your hat to great books with this reading motivation display! Have students read fiction books independently; then have each child complete a copy of the **book-review form** (page 153). Next, have each student create the hat she mentioned on her form using scrap paper and other art materials. Post the hats and forms on a bulletin board that will cause more than a few heads to turn!

Colleen Dabney—Grs. 6–7, Williamsburg Christian Academy, Williamsburg, VA

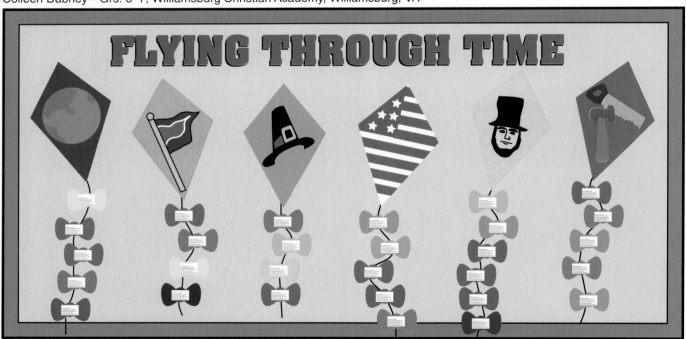

Watch summarizing skills soar with this high-flying display! After completing a unit in social studies or science, divide the textbook chapter into several sections. Assign one section to each group. Have the group summarize its section on an index card and then glue the card to a **bow pattern** (page 153). Finally, have each group design a kite that illustrates the chapter. Display the class's favorite kite with the bows as shown. Repeat this activity after each unit for an ongoing review.

Karen A. Jones—Gr. 4, Oxhead Road Elementary, Centereach, NY

Zip through a review of any topic with this interactive display. On the top half of a giant zipper cutout, post cards labeled with math problems. Place an envelope containing answer cards near the board. Then invite students to pin each problem's matching answer below it. Increase student involvement by having teams create new sets of cards to review other skills or topics.

Many students return to school wearing T-shirts that feature places they've visited or their favorite sports teams. Turn these shirts into a valuable learning experience and easy-to-make display. Copy the **T-shirt pattern** (page 154). Instruct each student to write the details about his T-shirt's origin on the pattern. Then have him turn over the pattern and decorate it to resemble his real shirt. Attach the completed shirts to the board with pushpins so they can easily be taken down and read by others.

Mary Chmelar—Gr. 4, Keota Community Schools, Keota, IA

It's no puzzle to see how this eye-catching—and simple—display reinforces the concept of symmetry. Have each student cut out a large puzzle piece from colorful paper. Then have him search through magazines to find an example of symmetry. After cutting out the example, the student glues it to his puzzle piece. Use this display idea to review other important skills such as numeration or parts of speech.

Colleen Dabney—Gr. 6, Williamsburg Christian Academy, Williamsburg, VA

Top tropical trees with tons of trivia during your next rain forest unit! Staple seven paper trunks labeled as shown to the board. Copy a large supply of leaves on green paper for students to cut out and place in a basket near the display. During the unit, have students label the leaves with facts they've learned and staple them atop the appropriate trunks.

Simone Lepine—Gr. 5, Gillette Road Middle School, North Syracuse, NY

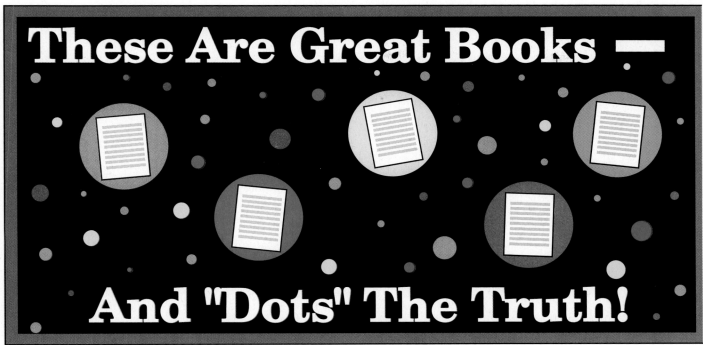

These Are Great Books —
And "Dots" The Truth!

Here's a board that will have your co-workers exclaiming, "Now 'dots' a great idea!" Have each student mount a book report on a large dot cut from neon-colored paper. Decorate the board further with smaller cut-out or self-sticking dots. Change the reports frequently to give students plenty of information about the great books "dot" are in your library!

Marilyn Gill, Noble, OK

Motivate your students to read with this sweet incentive! Challenge each child to read seven books of at least 100 pages each. Have the student's parents sign a slip verifying that the child has read each book. Each time a student brings in a book slip give him a miniature candy bar. After the student eats the candy, post the wrapper above his name on the board. Reward each student who reads all seven books with a giant candy bar and a certificate.

Philip Lang—Gr. 5
Christ Lutheran School
Rancho Palos Verde, CA

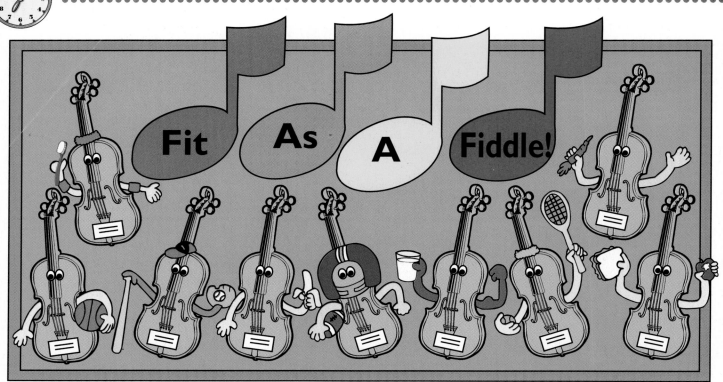

Tune in to the importance of good fitness and nutrition with this noteworthy display! On brown paper, make a class supply of the **fiddle pattern** (page 155). Have each student stick a file folder label to the bottom of his fiddle and label it with a good health reminder. Also have him glue cutout eyes to his fiddle. Finally, have the student use art materials to decorate his cutout to illustrate his good health reminder. Fit never looked finer!

This simple display invites students to share what they've learned. Write the name of each student on a library card pocket; then attach the pockets to the board. Provide each student with a copy of the **star pattern** (page 156) to decorate and mount near his pocket. Each week place a colored strip of paper inside every pocket. During that week, each child labels her strip with something she has learned; then she places the strip back in her pocket. At the end of the grading term, staple each student's strips together and send them home to his parents.

Lisa Curry—Gr. 4, River Oaks Baptist School, Houston, TX

74

You can bank on improving vocabularies with this interactive display! Label 24 green index cards with alphabet letters as shown. Punch a hole in the upper right corner of each card; then place the card on a metal ring. Mount the 24 rings on the board with pushpins. Punch holes in more blank cards. Store the cards in a basket labeled "Deposit Slips." When a student finds a new word in his reading, he writes it on a blank card; then he writes the definition and his name on the back of the card. The student adds, or deposits, the card into the word bank by placing it on the correct ring (behind the letter card). When you have a few extra minutes, take a ring from the board and review the words with students.

Marilyn Crenshaw—Gr. 4
David Elementary
The Woodlands, TX

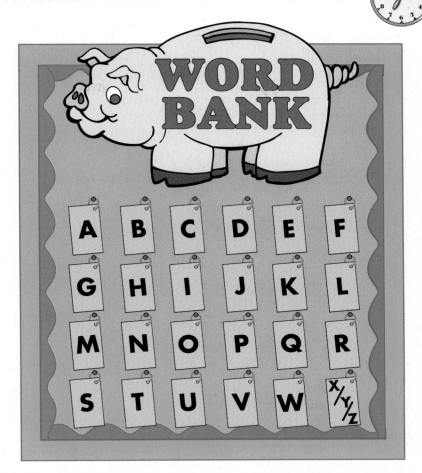

Promote reading with this easy-to-make display. Post an enlarged **book character pattern** (page 157) as shown. Have students work in pairs to create book jackets of their favorite humorous books to post on the board. Also allow students to use colorful markers to write their favorite one-line jokes or riddles directly on the background paper. Below each joke or riddle, the student adds the punch line or solution; then he staples a large index card on top to hide the answer. Encourage students to visit the board and enjoy each other's rib-ticklers!

Here's another piggy board that's packed with learning! Enlarge, color, and cut out the **pig pattern** (page 157). Laminate the pig and post it on a board as shown. Each week use a wipe-off marker to program the cutout with bonus spelling words. Have student groups use dictionaries to find the meanings of the words and write sentences using them. At the end of the week, review the words; then wipe the piggy clean so it's ready for next week's words! For fun, let your students suggest words to write on the piggy.

This creative-writing bulletin board is guaranteed to catch your students' fancy! Have each student color and cut out a **cat and cat tail pattern** (page 158) to attach to his complete "cat tale." Possible story starters include: "Turning into a cat seemed harmless until I…," "I nearly flipped when Catbo brought home a…," "My cat is so picky that…." Complete the display by adding a border of student-made paw prints.

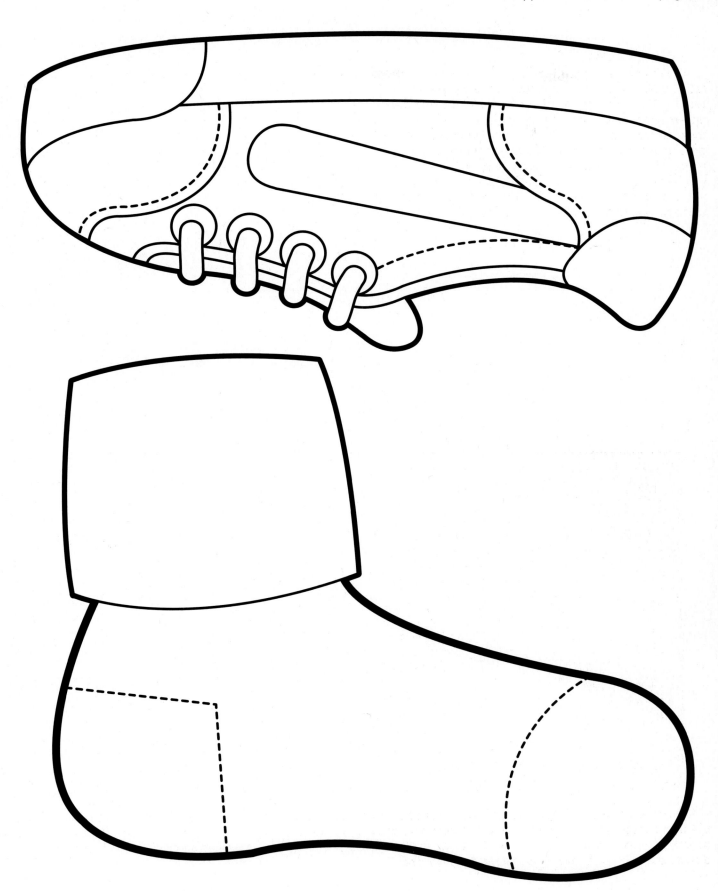

Patterns

Use with "Spend a Great Year in Fifth Grade!" on page 4.

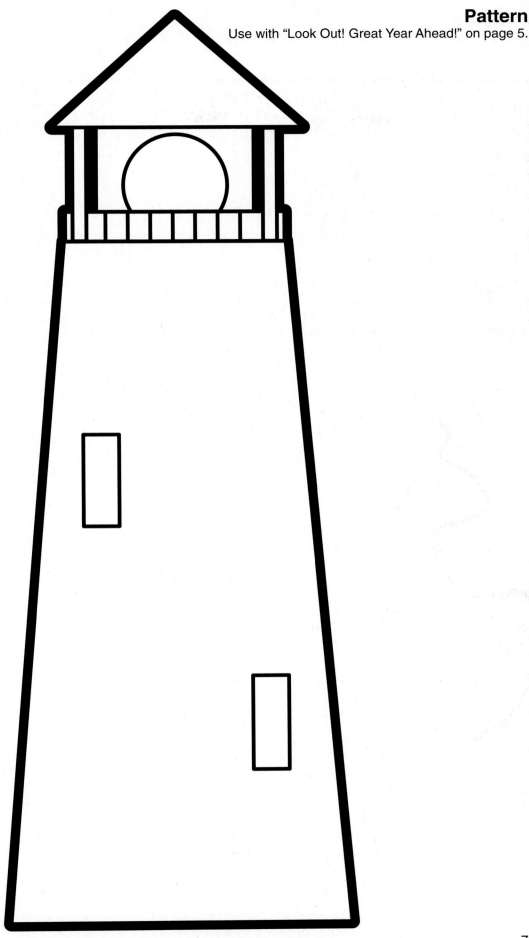

Pattern
Use with "Give a Cheer for a Great Year!" on page 5.

I'm Nuts About...

_____
student of the week

because _____

_____

_____

_____ .

Signed: _____

Pattern

Use with "Welcome Back From a First-Class Staff!" on page 6.

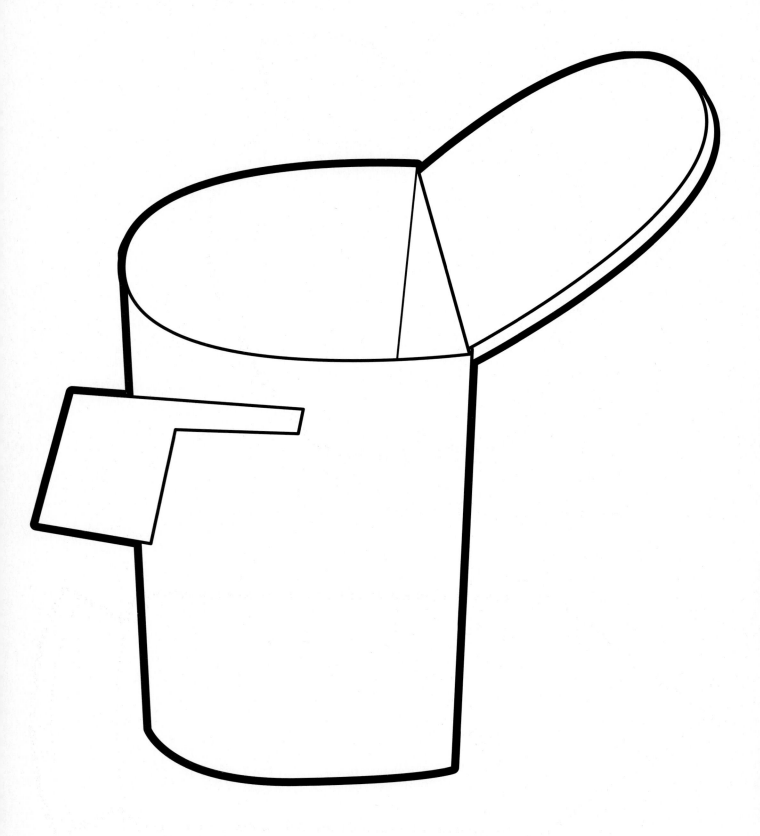

©The Education Center, Inc. • *The Best of* The Mailbox® *Bulletin Boards* • TEC60818

Patterns
Use with " 'Ap-peeling' Words of Wisdom" on page 7
and "Overall, It's Been a Great Year!" on page 40.

Use with "Fifth Graders Are out of This World!" on page 7.

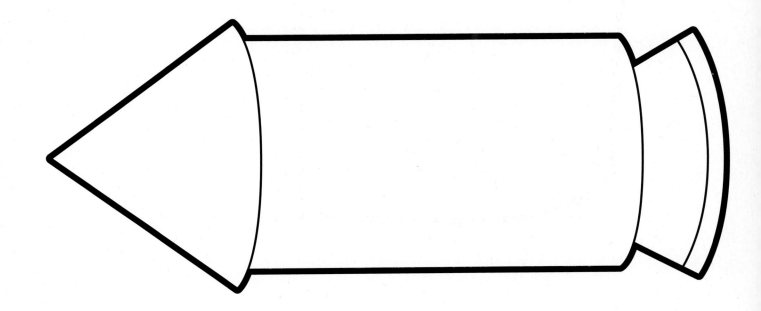

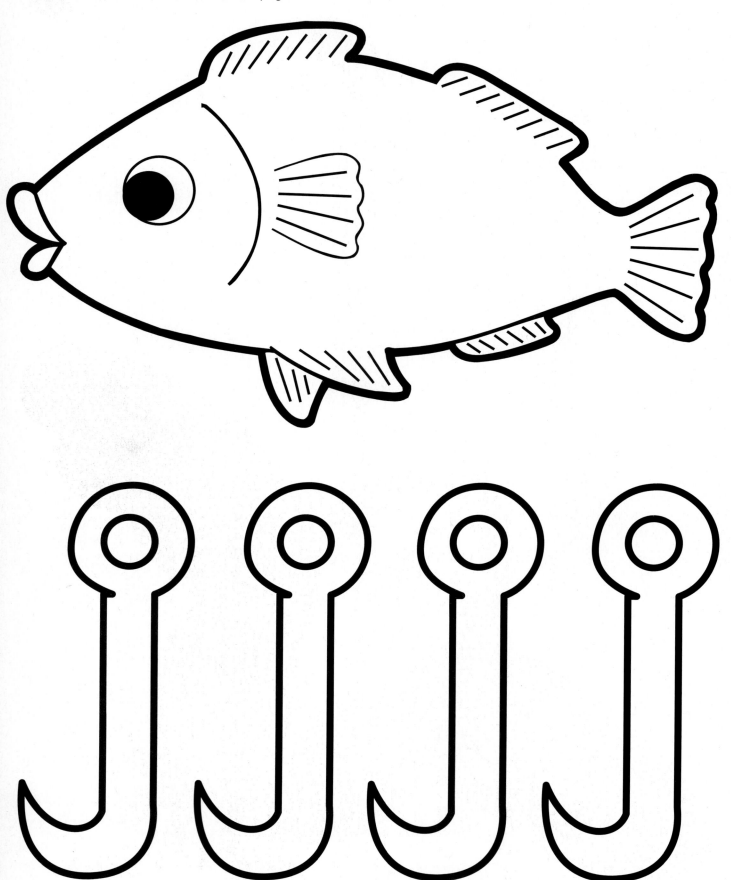

Use with "Something to Crow About!" on page 9.

Patterns

Use with "Treat Yourself to a Good Book!" on page 9.

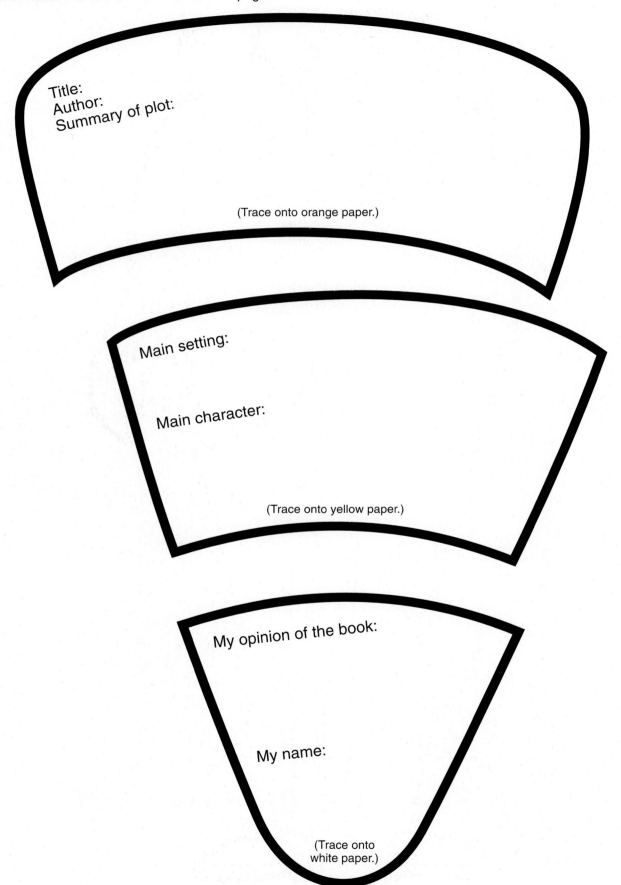

Title:
Author:
Summary of plot:

(Trace onto orange paper.)

Main setting:

Main character:

(Trace onto yellow paper.)

My opinion of the book:

My name:

(Trace onto white paper.)

Pattern
Use with "Pumpkin Personality Portraits" on page 10.

Pattern
Use with "Haunted Helpers" on page 11.

Use with "'Tie-m' to Give Thanks!" on page 13.

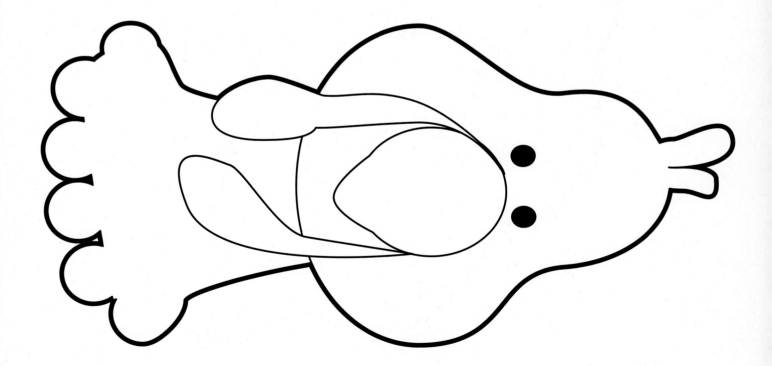

Pattern
Use with "Gobble Up a Great Book!"
on page 13.

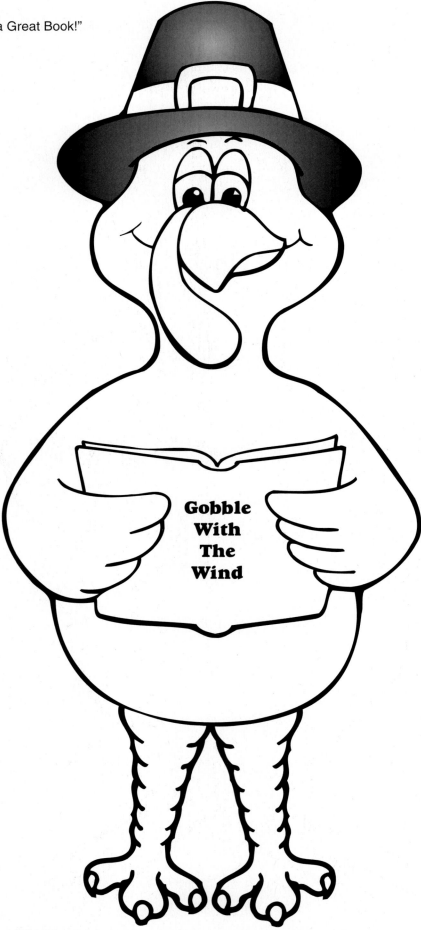

Gobble
With
The
Wind

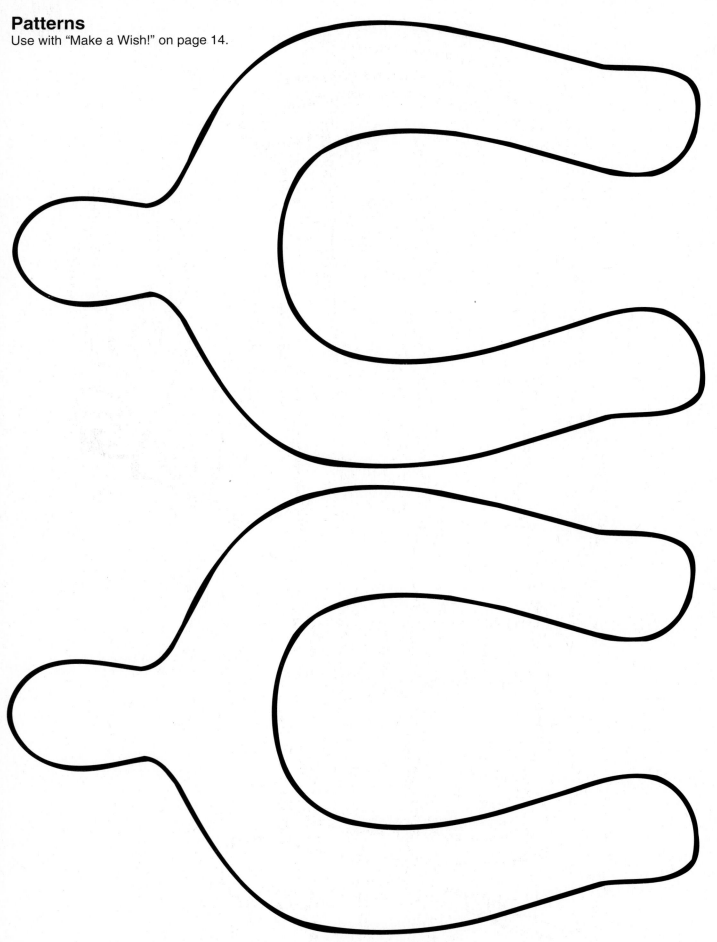

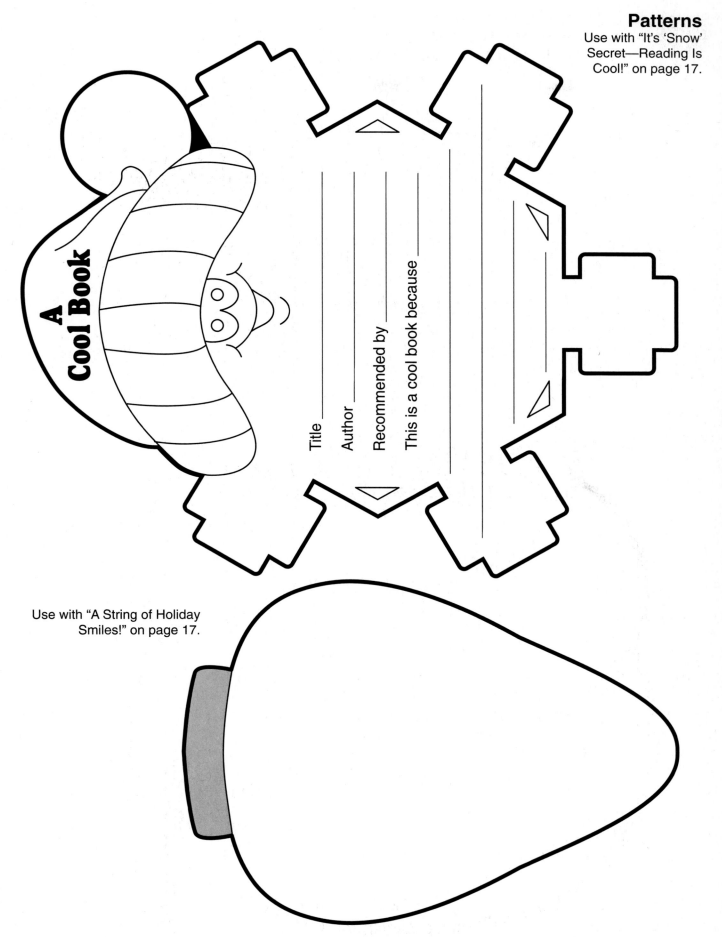

A Cool Book

Title _____

Author _____

Recommended by _____

This is a cool book because _____

Use with "A String of Holiday Smiles!" on page 17.

Patterns

Use with "Brighten Someone's Holiday Season!" on page 18.

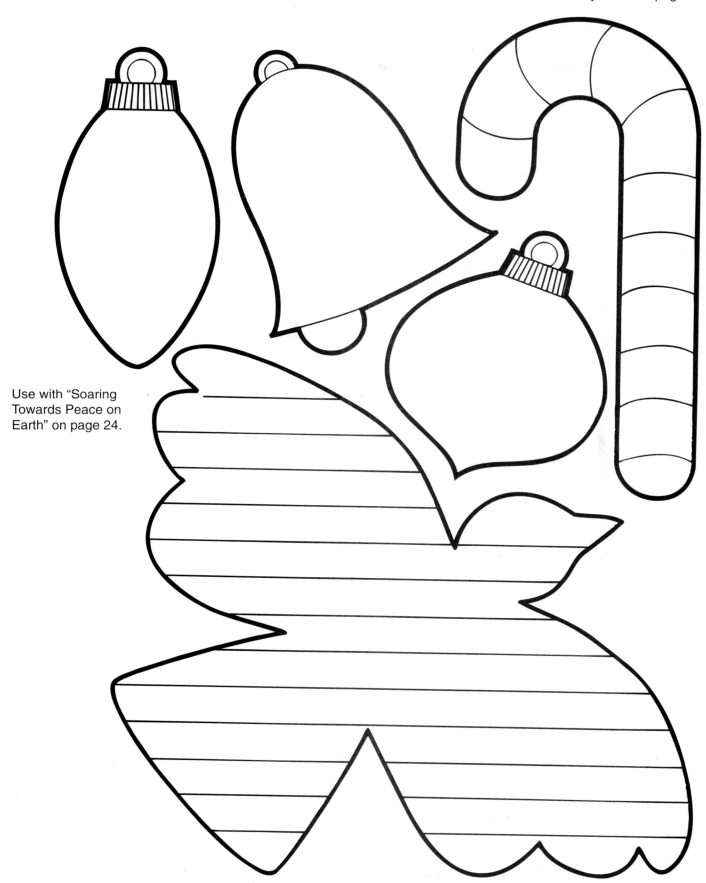

Use with "Soaring Towards Peace on Earth" on page 24.

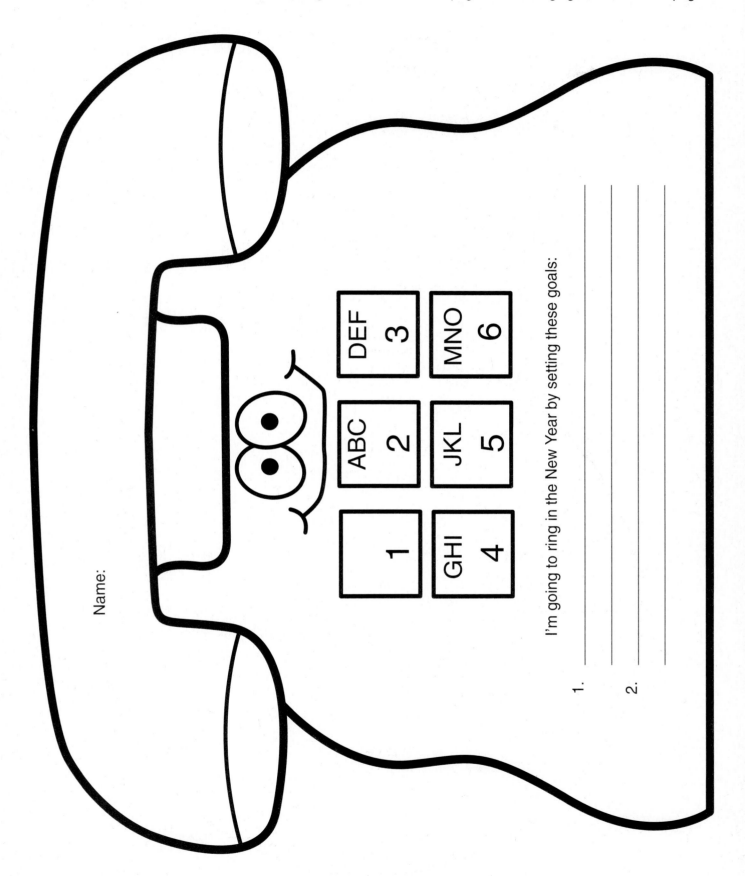

Name:

ABC 2

DEF 3

GHI 4

JKL 5

MNO 6

1

I'm going to ring in the New Year by setting these goals:

1.

2.

Pattern
Use with "Piecing Together African American History" on page 25.

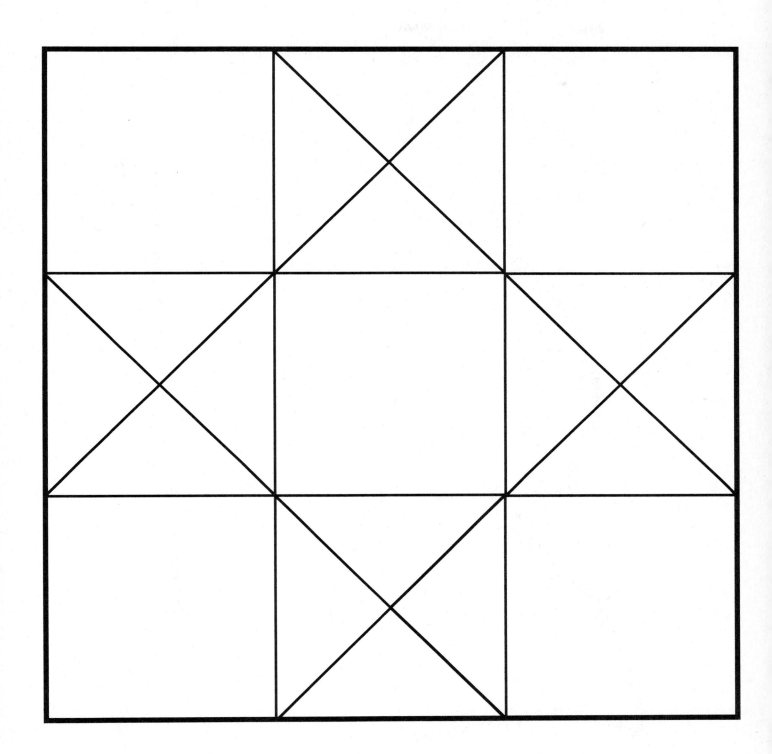

Patterns
Use with "Pouring Our Hearts Into Our Work!" on page 26.

Name:

♥♥♥♥♥♥♥♥♥♥♥♥

I can tell that I poured my heart into
this assignment because _____

_____
_____
_____
_____
_____
_____

♥♥♥

♥♥♥

_____
_____
_____
_____
_____
_____
_____

I can tell that I poured my heart into
this assignment because

♥♥♥♥♥♥♥♥♥♥♥♥

Name:

Patterns
Use with "Puppy Love" on page 27.

Pattern

Use with "Secret Shamrocks" and "Irish Eyes Are Smiling!" on page 30 and "Free Time? 'Tri' These!" on page 31.

Reading 'N' Riches

Book Report Form

Name: _____

Team: _____

Title of book: _____

Author: _____

Type of book: _____ No. of pages: _____

Write a brief summary of the book:

_____

_____

_____

_____

_____

_____

_____

_____

_____

_____

What would you like to change about this book?

_____

Rank the book from 1–10 by drawing gold coins in the space below. One coin indicates that you wouldn't recommend the book; 10 coins means it's one of the best books you've ever read.

©The Education Center, Inc. • *The Best of* The Mailbox® *Bulletin Boards* • TEC60818

Patterns
Use with "Out to Lunch!" on page 32.

Use with "We're So 'Hoppy' to Help!" on page 32.

Patterns

Use with "These Stories Are a Hit!" on page 34.

Use with "Fluttering Fractions" on page 33.

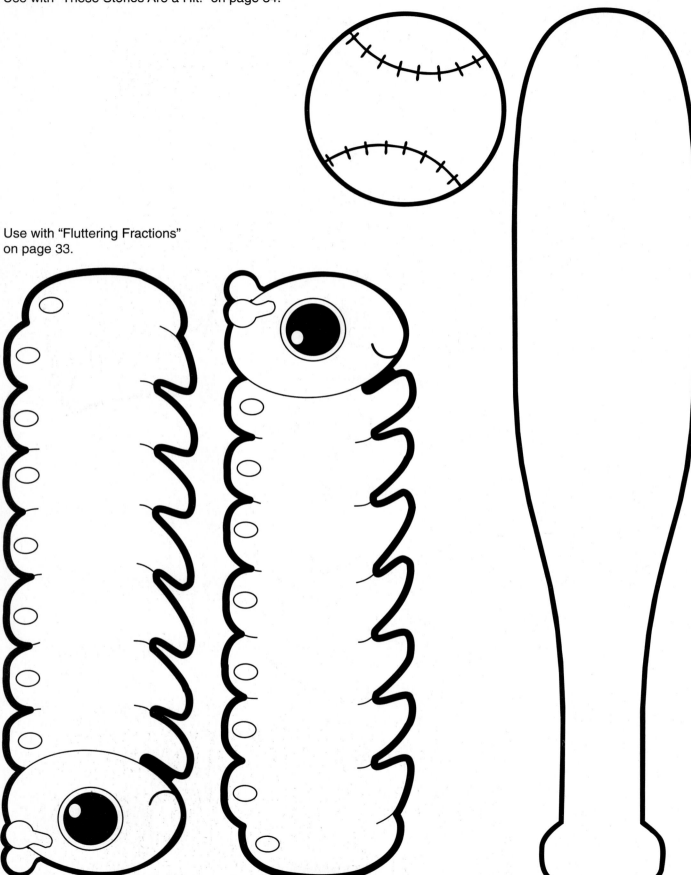

Patterns
Use with "Our Class Is Buzzing With Good Character!" on page 35.

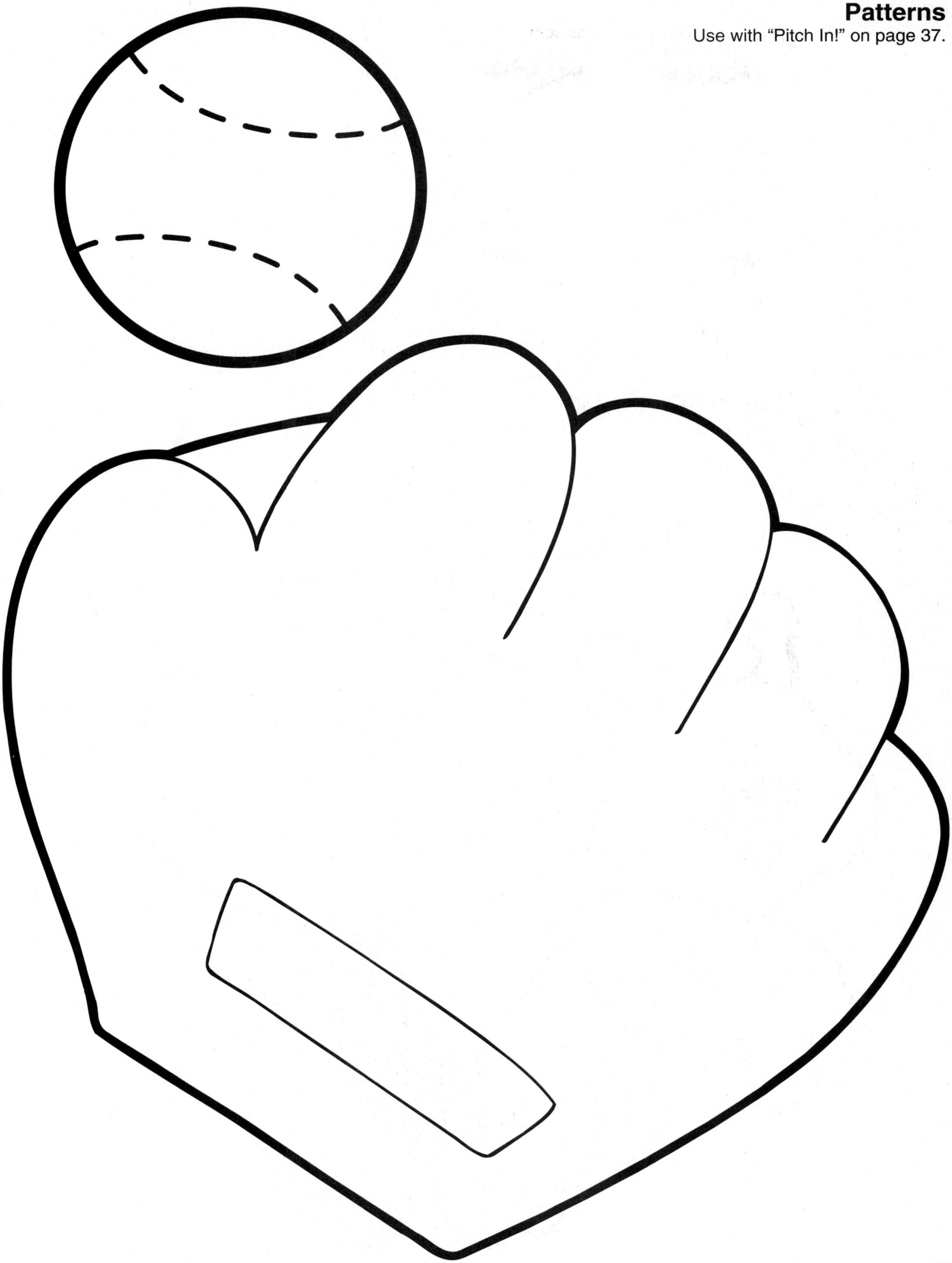

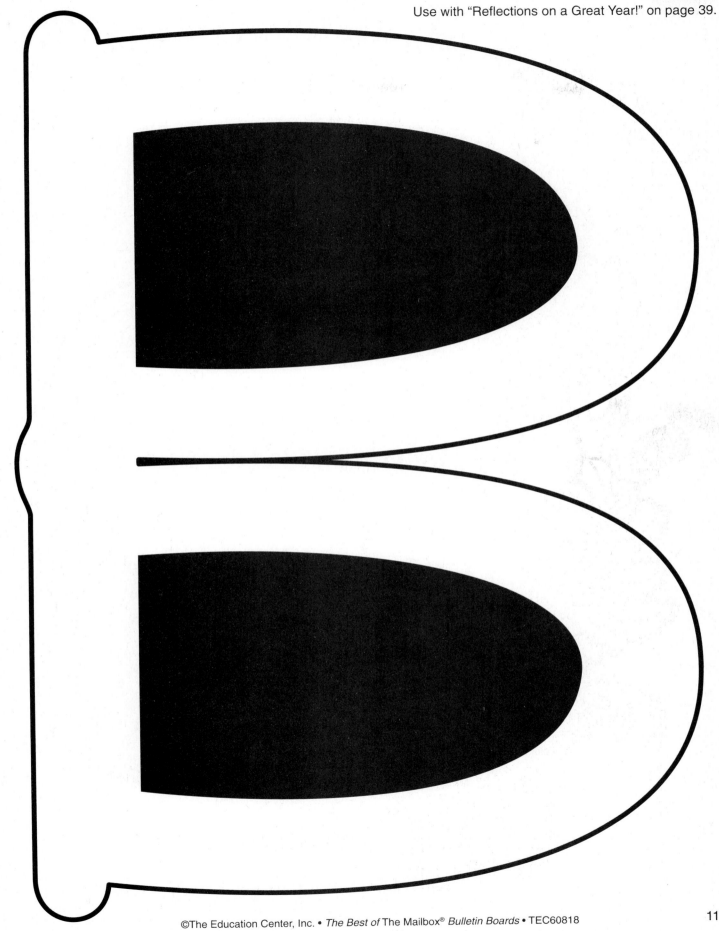

Patterns

Use with "'Orange' You Glad You Were in 5th Grade?" on page 40.

Use with "Fifth Grade Was a Flock of Fun!" on page 41.

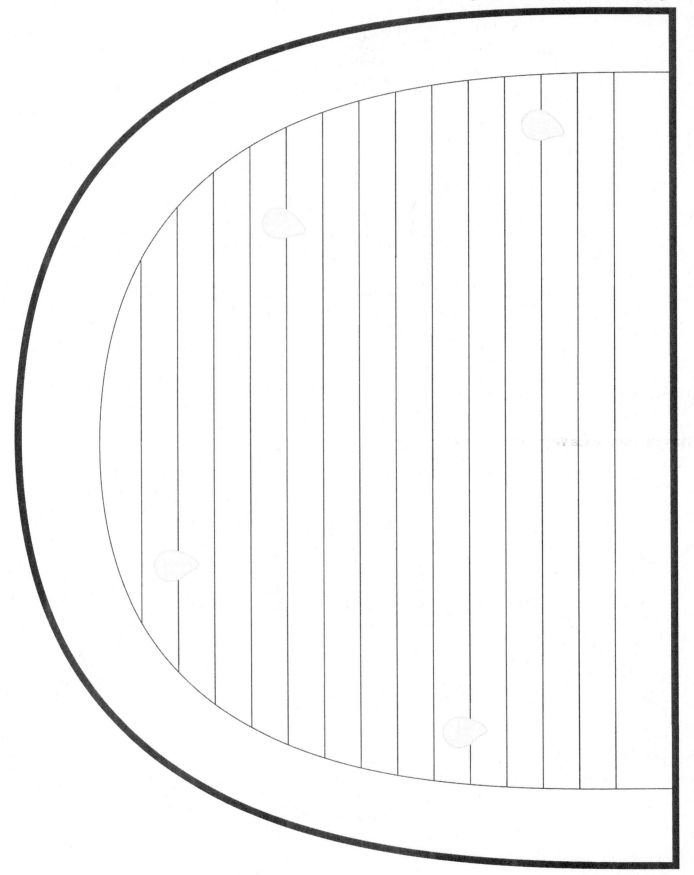

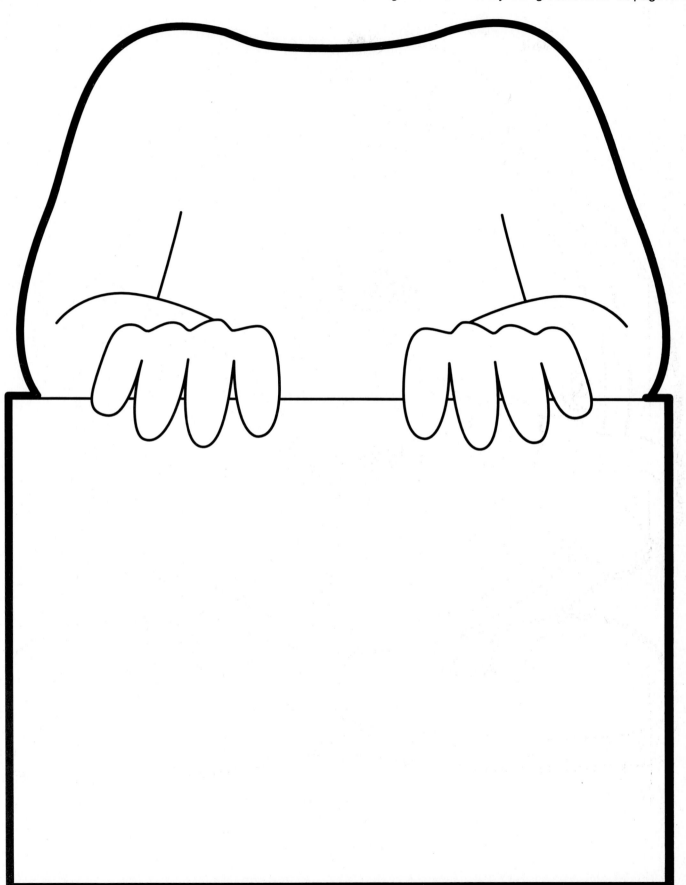

Use with "We've Been Spotted Working Hard!" on page 48.

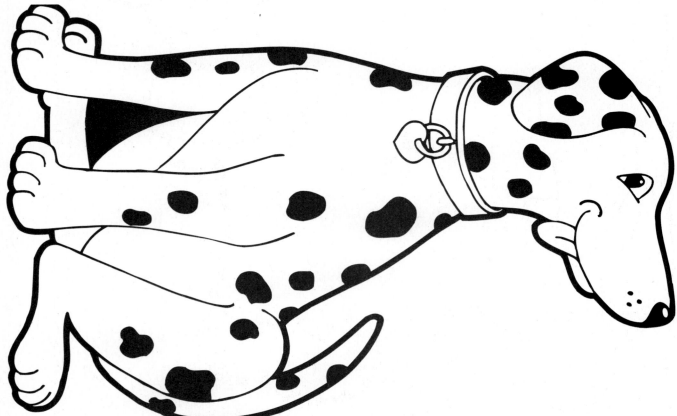

Pattern
Use with "Don't Parrot Platitudes—Act!" on page 51.

Patterns

Use with "Squeak a Peek…at Our Week!" on page 54.

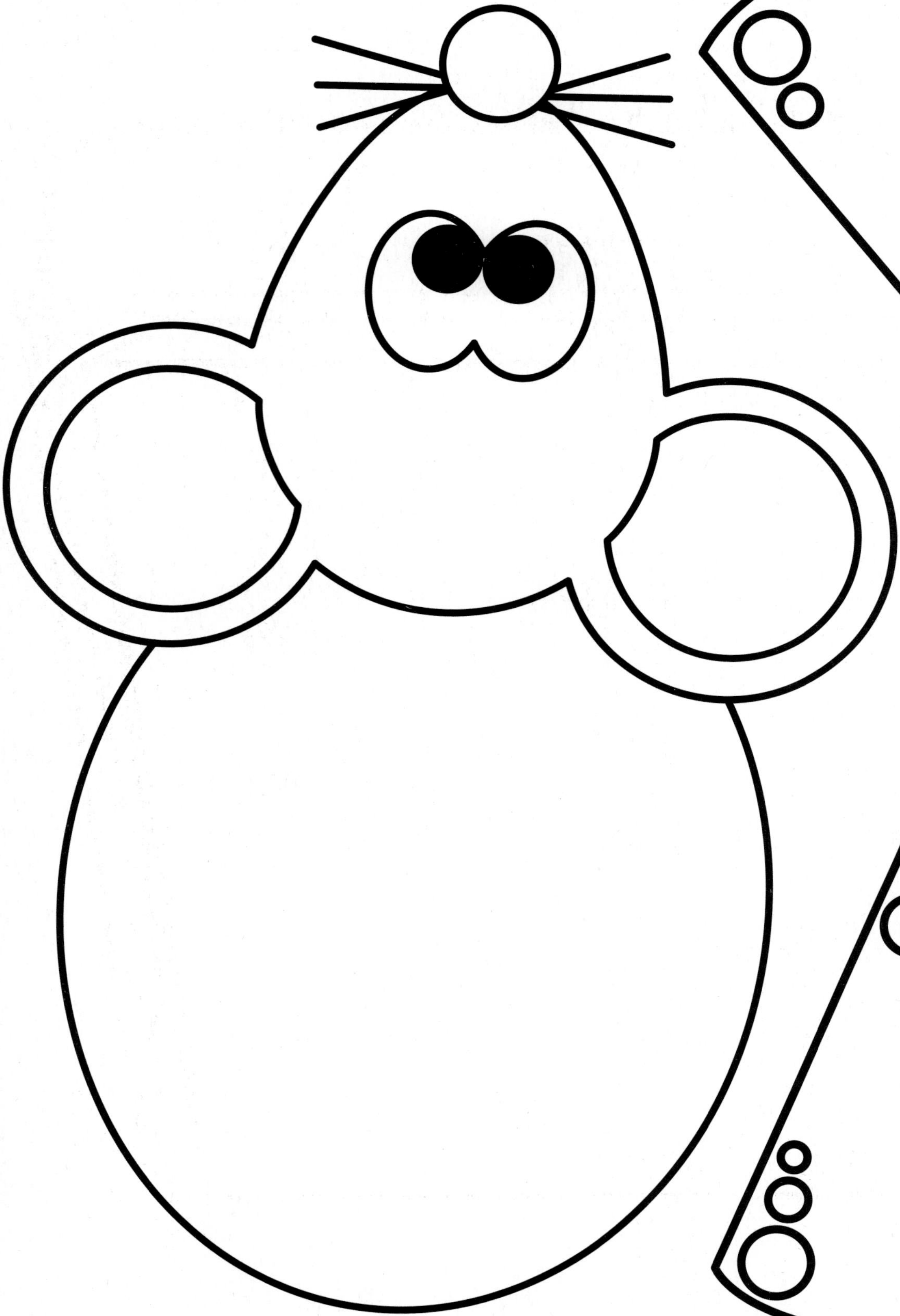

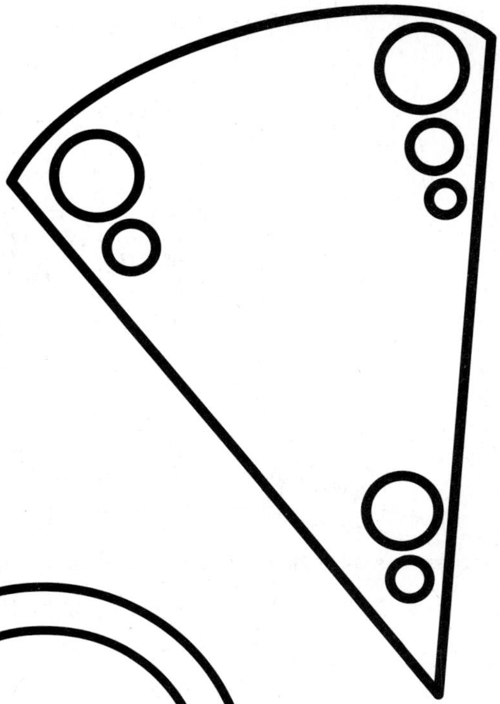

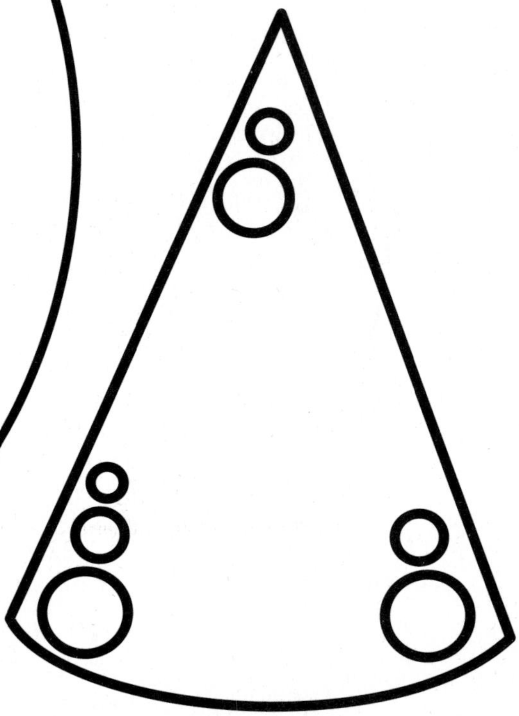

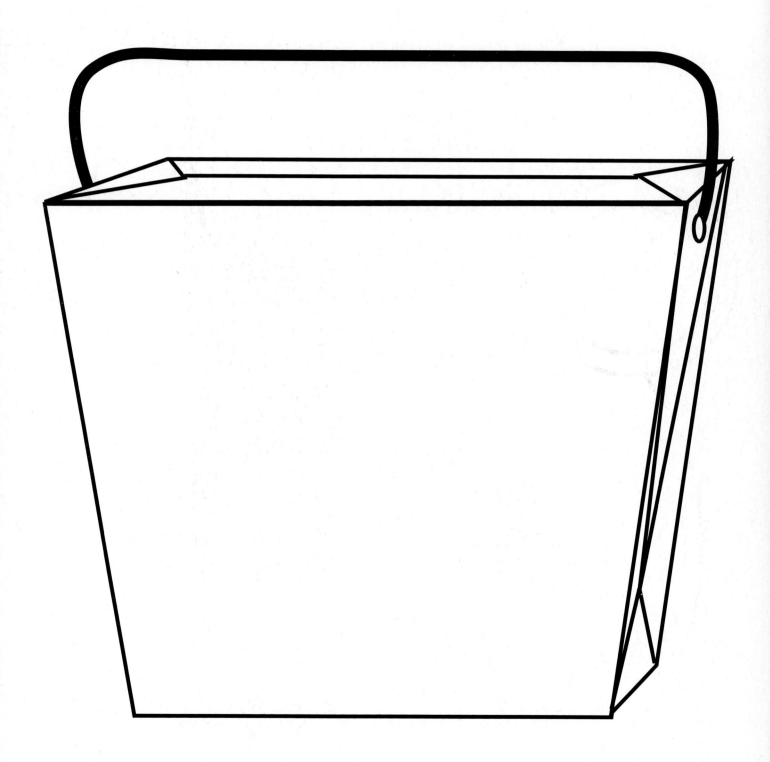

Patterns

Use with "The Party Animal" on page 55.

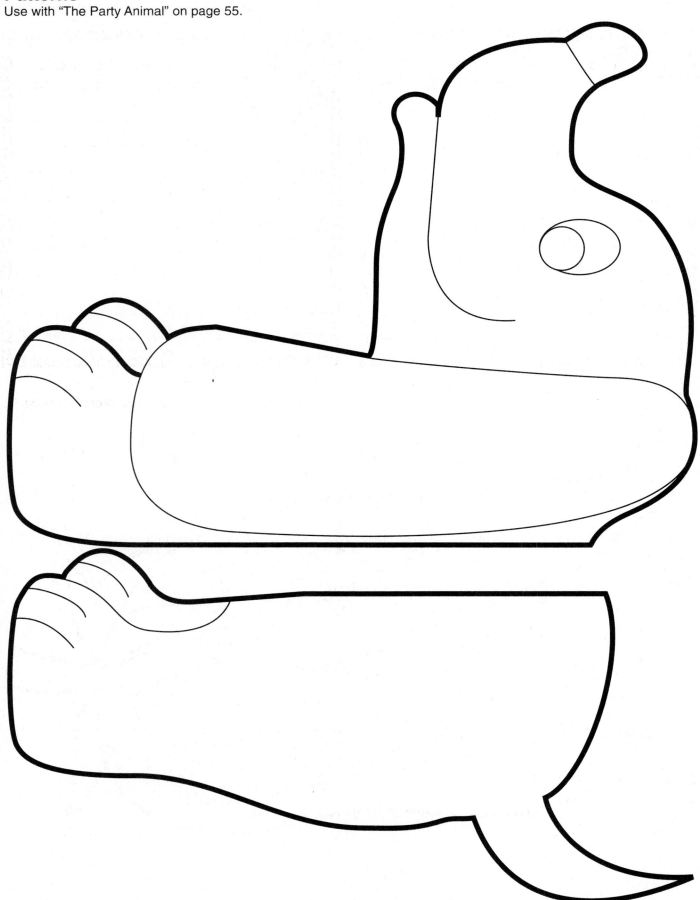

I'm spotlighting this assignment because

_____

_____

_____

_____

_____

_____

_____

Name _____

Date _____

©The Education Center, Inc.

I'm spotlighting this assignment because

_____

_____

_____

_____

_____

_____

_____

Name _____

Date _____

©The Education Center, Inc.

Use with "Hot Work!" on page 57.

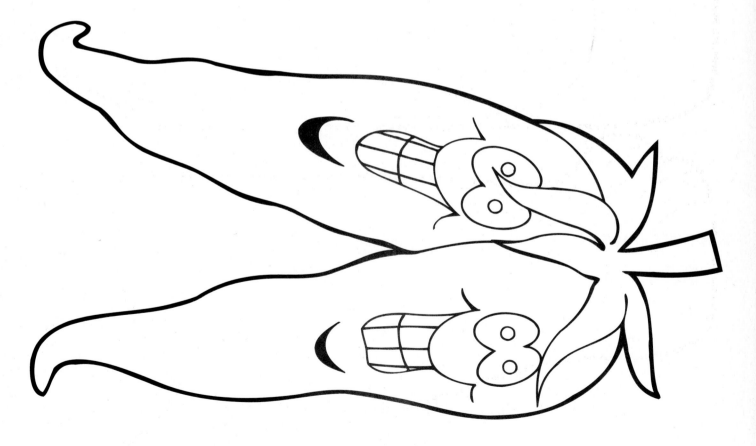

Patterns

Use with "Our Artwork Makes a Splash!" on page 58.

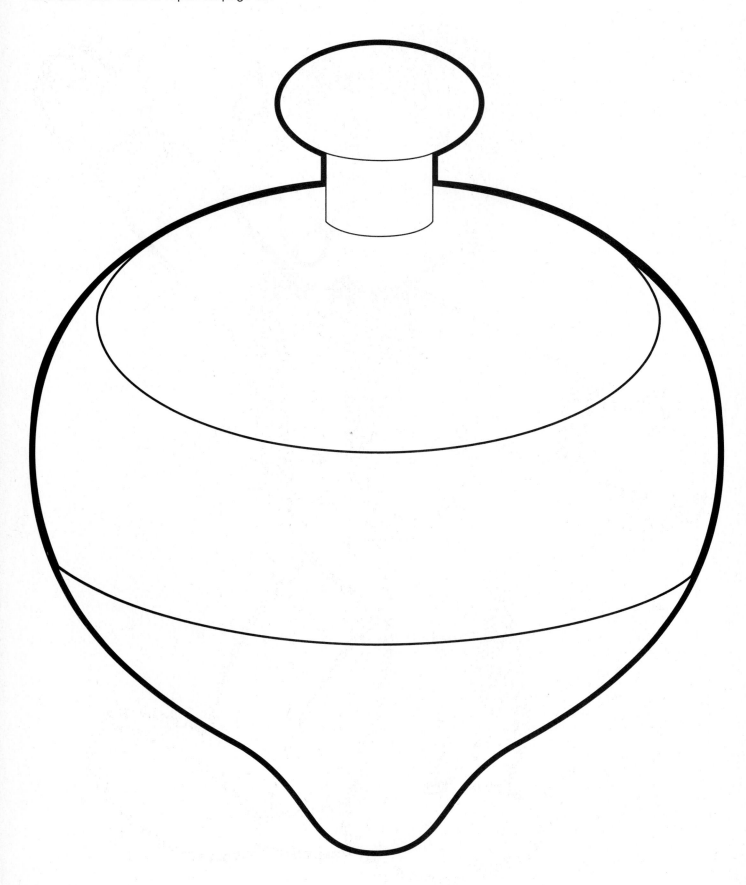

Pattern

Use with "For Great 'Purr-formances'—Do Your Best!" on page 59.

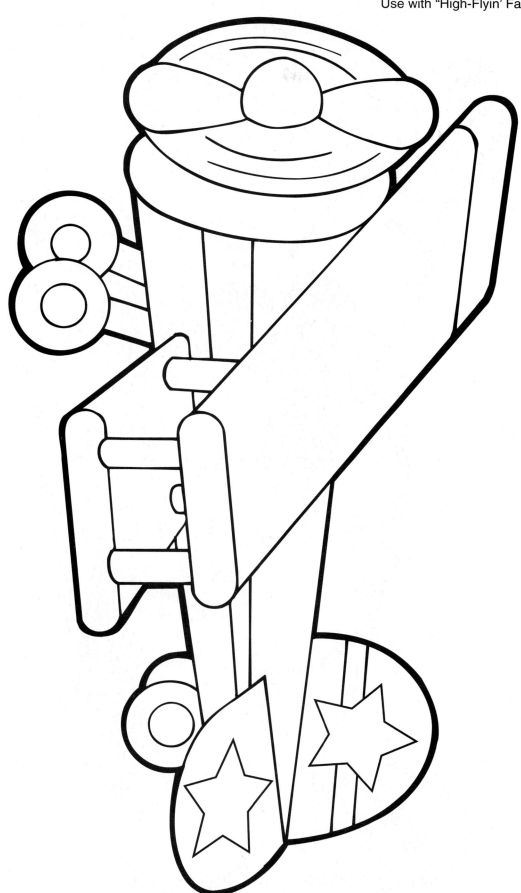

Pattern
Use with "Pieces of Our Lives" on page 61.

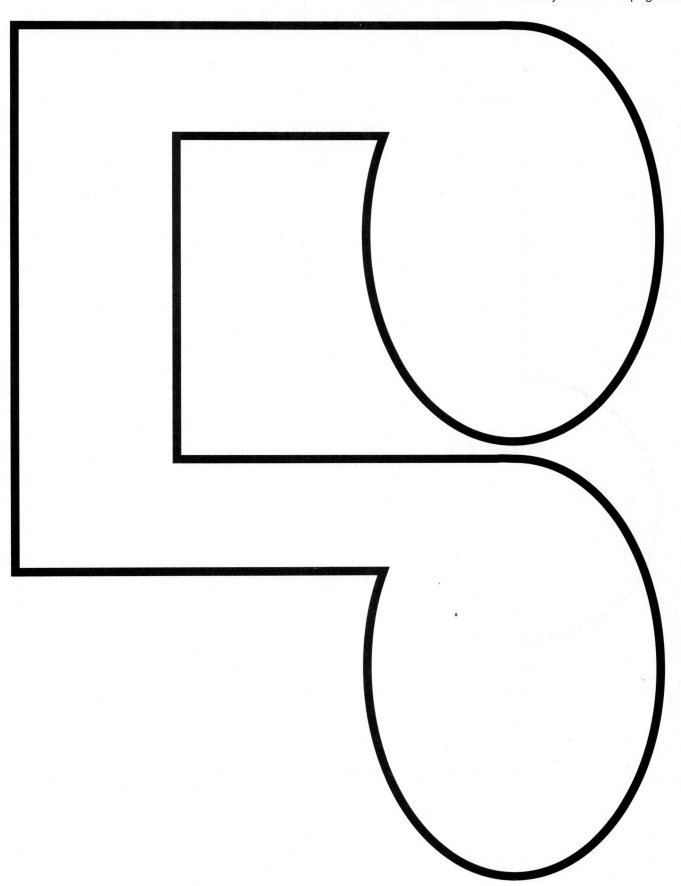

Patterns
Use with "Fishin' for a Solution!" on page 62.

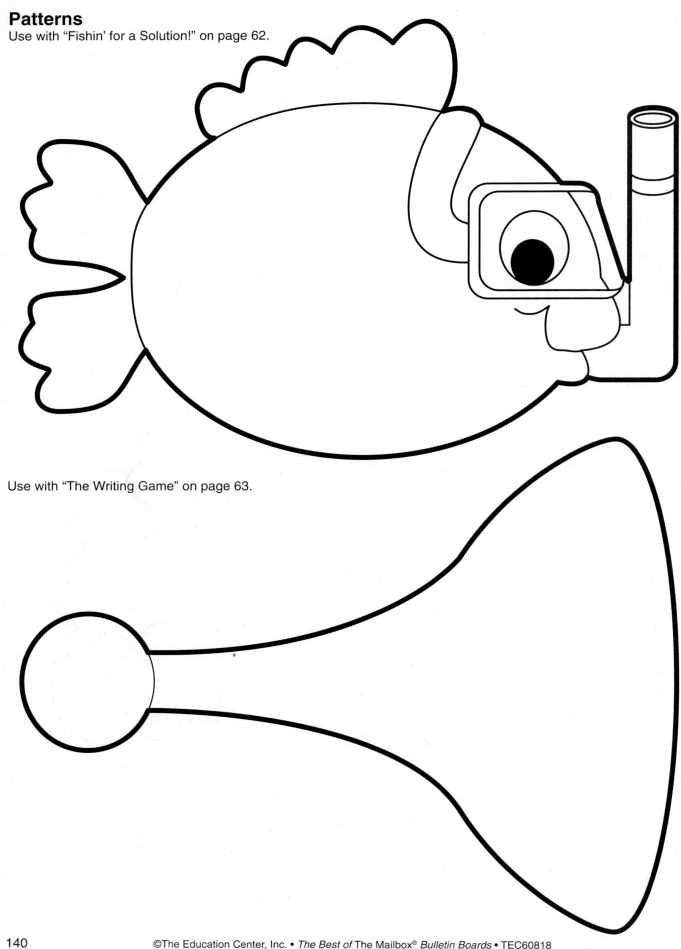

Use with "The Writing Game" on page 63.

Pattern
Use with "Boning Up on Science" on page 64.

Use with "Boning Up on Science" on page 64.

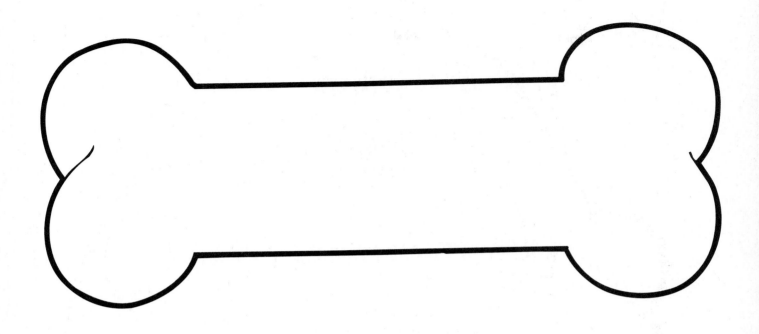

Use with "Paging All Readers" on page 64.

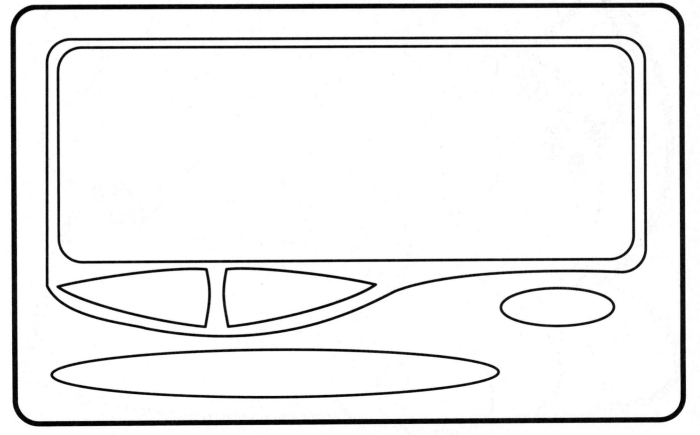

Pattern
Use with "Brush Up on Facts!" on page 65.

Patterns

Use with "Brush Up on Facts!" on page 65.

Use with "Great Spelling Is a Go!" on page 65.

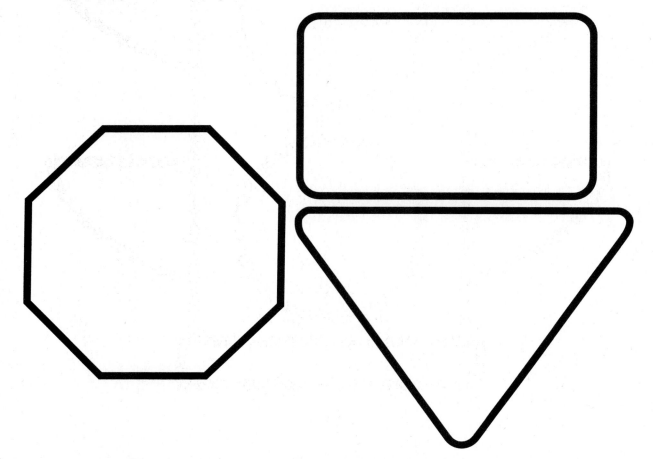

Patterns

Use with "Shoot for the Stars!" on page 66.

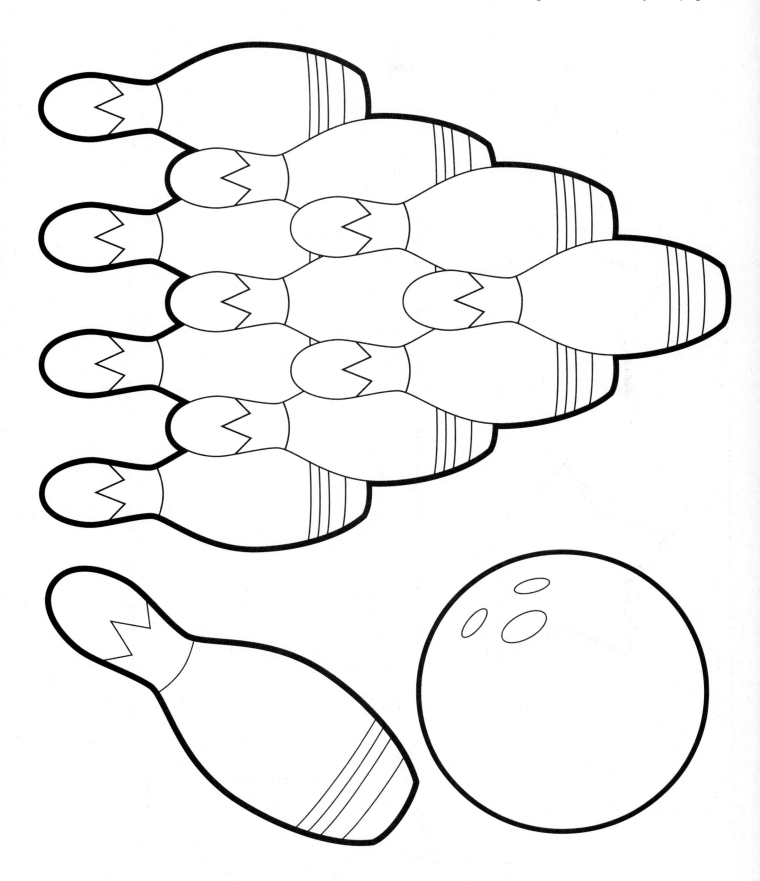

Patterns

Use with "Wrap Your Arms Around These Good Books!" on page 68.

Wrap Your Arms Around These Good Books!

This booklist belongs to

Ten books recommended by my classmates that I'd like to read:

1.
2.
3.
4.
5.
6.
7.
8.
9.
10.

Other Great Books to Grab!

- *The Castle in the Attic* by Elizabeth Winthrop
- *The Ballad of Lucy Whipple* by Karen Cushman
- *The View From Saturday* by E. L. Konigsburg
- *There's a Boy in the Girls' Bathroom* by Louis Sachar
- *Knights of the Kitchen Table* by Jon Scieszka
- *Turn Homeward, Hannalee* by Patricia Beatty
- *Ella Enchanted* by Gail Carson Levine
- *Redwall* by Brian Jacques
- *The Wolves of Willoughby Chase* by Joan Aiken
- *Poppy* by Avi
- *The Missing 'Gator of Gumbo Limbo: An Ecological Mystery* by Jean Craighead George
- *Trouble River* by Betsy Byars

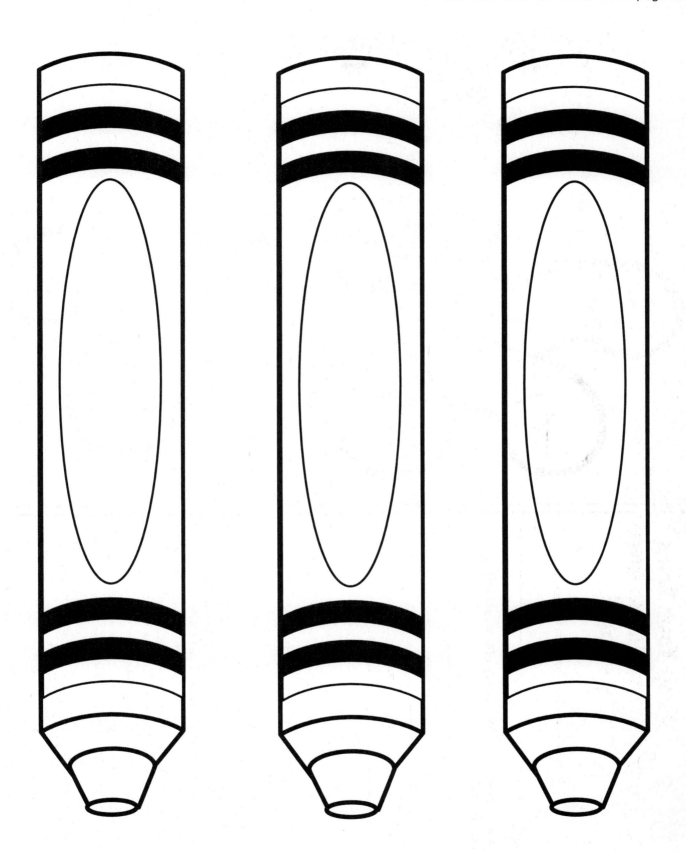

Patterns

Use with "The Right Combination" on page 69.

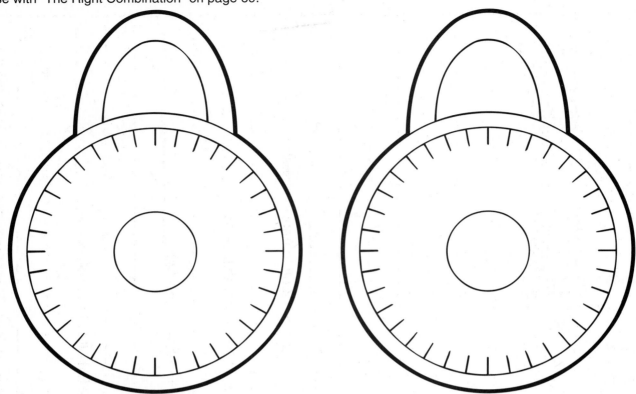

Use with "Ask the Expert!" on page 69.

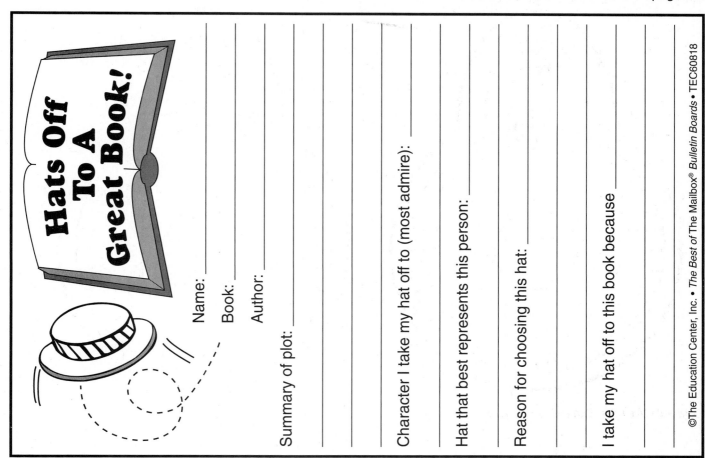

Name:

Book:

Author:

Summary of plot:

Character I take my hat off to (most admire):

Hat that best represents this person:

Reason for choosing this hat:

I take my hat off to this book because

©The Education Center, Inc. • *The Best of* The Mailbox® *Bulletin Boards* • TEC60818

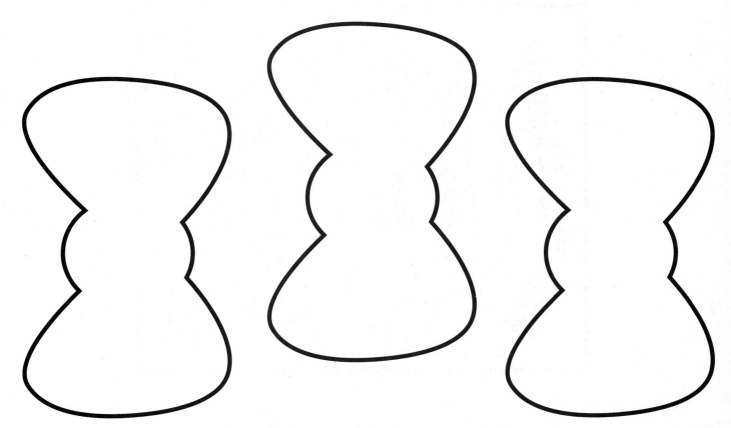

Pattern

Use with "Where in the World Did You Get That Shirt?" on page 71.

Where in the WORLD did you get that SHIRT?

____

It is ________________________ of our community.
(direction)

The climate in this place is ____________________
____.

The land in this place is ______________________
____.

Three interesting facts I learned about this place:

1. ____________________________________
   ____
2. ____________________________________
   ____
3. ____________________________________
   ____

This place is located near ____________ latitude and ____________ longitude.

Name____________________________________

Pattern
Use with "Look What We've Learned!" on page 74.

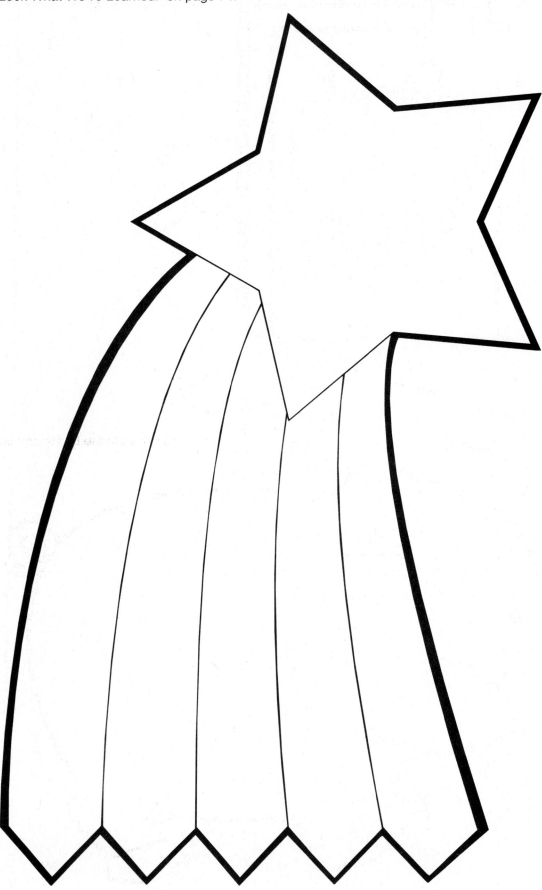

Use with "This Little Piggy Went to the Dictionary" on page 76.

Patterns
Use with "'Purr-fectly' Wonderful Cat Tales" on page 76.

Index